X-MAN:
GOD'S NEW CREATURE

X-MAN:

GOD'S NEW CREATURE

X-MAN the CHRIST-MAN
If any man be in Christ, he is a new creature [X-Man];
old things are passed away; behold, all things have become new.
2 Corinthians 5:17

Edward O'Neal Benson

Lord you said you could use anyone, BUT can you use me?

To order additional copies of this book, contact:
Xlibris Corporation
1-888-795-4274
www.Xlibris.com
Orders@Xlibris.com
32977

CONTENTS

DEDICATION

This book is dedicated in memory of my spiritual father, Rev. C. D. Tate who served as my Pastor at First Temple Church of Christ Holiness, U.S.A. in Brookhaven, Mississippi for Sixteen years. He poured everything he had into me especially his wisdom and knowledge of the word. He opened his home to me while I was attending Millsap's College in Jackson, Mississippi. When I couldn't afford to live in the college dormitory or afford the meal plan to eat in the cafeteria, he showed genuine love. Rev. Tate always knew that one day I would preach God's word. Thus, he along with the entire Church of Christ Holiness Denomination made certain I had a solid foundation in Christ. His favorite songs, "How Great Thou Art" and "He Touched Me" still reverberate deep within my soul. I have no doubt that he is looking from Heaven smiling knowing that Jesus has touched me and now I am no longer the same.

In his ministry Reverend Tate expressed that we all come to God with hurts, habits and hang-ups. Yet because Christ died for our sins we can all be transformed and live a life of freedom and redemption.

ACKNOWLEDGEMENTS

I thank God for guiding my life and allowing me the opportunity to walk in my calling as an X-Man.

To my Pastor, Ronald O. Perry, Sr. of Springfield Baptist Church, Beacon, New York who inspired the title of this book. Thank you for your prayers, teachings and daily example of Godly "X-Man" living and for re-opening my eyes to discern the truth that can only be found in Christ Jesus. Because of you and the Springfield family, I am able to walk in my calling. I now strive to follow Rev. Perry's ministry as Elisha followed Elijah hoping that God will bless me one day with a double portion of the spirit I see working in him.

To my former Pastor, Terrell Brinson and the men of Brookhaven Living Word Christian Center, Brookhaven, Mississippi, I wish to express my gratitude for the fellowship that began this project.

To my mother, Beulah D. Benson, now deceased, thanks for sending me to church. To Mary Jane Dillon my Aunt who always saw me as the man God wanted me to be. We should all be blessed to have such devoted people in our lives.

I wish to express my thanks to Phillip Sterling, Bruce Smith and other Pastors and Ministers of Lincoln County, Mississippi and Pastor John Hooks of Marlboro, NY who encouraged me every opportunity they could get. To my friends in the Fourteen Circuit Court District, Mahundis Brice, and especially the local attorneys and judges who always expressed a genuine concern that God had his hand on me.

To my brother Abdullah, thanks for sending monthly words of encouragement and insight. I thank God for your ministry.

To my baby sister Diane (an X-Woman) thanks for having faith in me, as I have faith in you. God has a place for you to serve and be served.

A special thanks to my sisters Margaretta, Helen, Laura and Shirley and my great friend Natasha Haynes for always believing in me and cheering me on.

For her wisdom, comments and perceptive criticism and support of earlier drafts of this book, I would like to express my gratitude to my sister, Minister Luader Smith, associate Minister of Springfield Baptist Church and Executive Director of House of Faith Ministry, Inc. And a special thanks to Julius P. Smith for keeping me in his prayers.

I thank my deceased father and brother, R.W. Benson, Sr. and R.W. Benson, Jr. I am grateful and at peace that both of you became X-Men and died before you Died-I look at your life's end and I am inspired.

I extend my most sincere and heartfelt thanks to my friend Ren Brown, a man of great passion and commitment to friendship. I thank you for your interest and caring at a time when it would have been a whole lot easier not to.

To Connie Lamar, Carine Lindor and Deacon Eugene Reilly thanks for your assistance with the cover and other photos for this book. God brought each of you into my life at the right time.

I am particularly indebted to and thank God for Rita Ihekwaba, who carefully read the entire manuscript, putting her vast knowledge at my disposal. Her suggestions and wisdom are reflected at many points throughout the book and helped in a significant way to raise the level of accuracy, readability and insight.

I must say, despite the wealth of help I received, I alone am responsible for any errors that remain.

To Deborah Benson thank you for watching over my blessings from God while they are in your care. I am immensely grateful for your support.

To my beloved children: Adrienne, Malik, Christen, Tiffany and Alexander, I would like to express my deepest appreciation for each of you. It has been my love for each of you that has helped me carry this project to its completion that I might become an example for each of you to be proud of.

Finally, but immensely, to my wife Aisha, my best friend, my love, my confidante, and safe harbor in the storm, I must give you special thanks, for believing in my dream and for proof reading the numerous drafts of this book in a way that most writers can only dream about. Thank you for sharpening my prose and making the book accessible to a broad audience. May God's grace be with you always.

X-MAN DEFINED

X-Man: A Christ-Man. A Man of God; A New Creature in Christ; A Man who had put aside his sins to follow Christ, who is evolving daily to becoming a new man in Christ, who has transformed his character and behavior and accepted his calling to work and recruit for Christ; An anointed man of God.

INTRODUCTION

X-MAN—God's new creature

"The Evolution of Man"

From the above definition of the X-Man, the reader will gather that this book is not about comic book characters or mythical creatures or half superhero-half human hybrids. It is a book about men who are very real and very human. Men who choose to break through a past of pain, doom and despair, condemnation, humiliation, degradation and a socialization process that teaches them to suppress emotions, to strive for power and riches, to dominate women, to lie, steal and cheat, to be macho, to be lead by their ego, to get ahead at all costs, to be their own gods, and to live the life of a rap video or R-Rated movie.

When people first hear the name X-Man, they first think of the comic book characters from Marvel Comics. They think about Professor Charles Xavier, Wolverine, Iceman, Storm, Phoenix, Magneto and Mystique. They even go so far to mention other comic book characters such as Daredevil, Spiderman and even Superman. Most fictional superheroes have undergone a physical mutation process that granted them some special super powers. It is my hope that one day all Christians will pick up their cross of transformation and realize that we all have the power to become X-Men and X-Women for Christ.

Most men when choosing to overcome have acknowledged their sinful nature by wanting to become a new man in Christ. However, they may not know where to begin or how to stay on track. Or perhaps they want a better understanding of the root of the problem or want to know when they have at last reached the road's end. This book aims to aid the X-man along his journey and provide insight on why the transformation must take place, and serve as a roadmap on the journey. Regardless of where each man is in his transformation process, this book will help.

In addition to guidelines for everyone to live by, this book also outlines some of my personal struggles and transformation from sinner to X-Man. It is my way through Christ to allow my past to be used to advance the gospel. It is my desire for each reader to come face to face with himself (as a real man) to consider the roots of his past and form a generalized mental picture of the exterior physical world with him in it as an X-Man. I believe as we begin to read, discuss and understand the bible and pray, we will begin to understand ourselves as well as God's desired purposes for our lives.

This book looks at the emotions, integrity and pride of man as it reminds each reader to take responsibility for the salvation of his own soul. With our technology advancing by leaps and bounds, one can say almost anything about human culture now and it will be true. Yet one thing is not advancing in America. Men are still not able to grow together. In a world filled with problems, confusion, misery, infidelity, disrespect, high levels of incarceration with little hope of rehabilitation, drug abuse, irresponsibility and other evils, we've taken every conceivable male bonding condition to extremes so as not to destroy barriers that are keeping so many from finding their calling in the Lord.

Just as God used twelve steps to complete the creation of the Universe and Man, I have penned twelve sessions of discussion on the creation, new birth and evolving transformation of X-Men. The bible states that the earth was without form and void (just as our lives are without God) until the spirit of God moved upon it. First, God said, "Let there be light" and this created (1) 'day" and (2) "night". Then God created (3) the earth and (4) the Sea. He (5) let the earth bring forth grass, the herb yielding seed and fruit trees (vegetation), (6) let there be lights from signs and seasons. Then God made two great lights (7) the greater to rule the day and (8) the lesser to rule the night. Then He said,(9) let the waters bring forth living creatures and (10) the fowl (birds) to fly above the earth. (11) Let the earth bring forth-living creatures. And finally,(12) God said, "let us make man in our own image, after our likeness". Let us make X-Man.

This Book will cause you to ponder some straightforward biblical teachings whose deeper meaning is often overlooked. For example, why were there three crosses on Calvary and not ten or twelve, or why was Jesus in the middle and not on the left or right end. In my opinion, it was because the three crosses represented choice and free will. Both criminals were tried and convicted by the same court system and condemned to the same crucifixion and yet, each had equal access to Jesus. Isn't it amazing how two people can hear the same story or be faced with the same life changing circumstances and make different choices? One turns away in mocking hatred, while the other worships and says "I believe". While one of the criminals continued to insult Jesus with the crowd, the other asked Jesus to remember him when he comes into His kingdom. This man, despite all of his mistakes, finally made a good choice at the end of his life. This is evidence that sometimes your worst moment is the prelude to your best. Midnight is just before day. Joy does come in the morning. Your X can become your cross to deliverance, but you must make the choice.

It is my hope that each reader will gain a sense of knowing the power of God and the direction he desires for his life. Each reader has an opportunity to become a great man or woman, but each person must first take a stand and choose whom he or she will serve. Growing old is inevitable. Growing UP in Christ is optional.

In the end, after God has humbled you by stripping you of the very thing that has made you what and who you are in the world, it still remains your sovereign choice, your right whether or not you become members of the X-Men.

But before we push play, let's pause for a moment so all of the facts are straight. This book is about men and for men, but women will benefit from reading it because the transformation process is equally applicable to women's lives. God can divert your agonies into victory and prosperity. He will take away hardship and give you joy. As you strive to understand and deal with the men in your lives, it will assist women who wish to meet the **perfect man on earth, a good man one who is reachable and teachable-an X-Man.** As you transform into an X-woman, just like Rahab in the book of *Joshua*, when the enemy comes he will find that you are not the woman you used to be. As it was with Rahab, who was rehabilitated and transformed as a direct result of her new belief and faith, your **entire** house can be saved.

SESSION ONE

The Transformation Begins
A New Creature In Christ By Beholding

True Transformation

You fill my heart and head with daring dreams of radical reforms,
Calling me to true transformation,
And still I struggle with simple steps,
Paralyzed by pain of paper-cut proportion,
Sulking in my own selfishness,
A ship sunk in sin.
Yet I believe the dreams you plant will prosper,
I will sail through the struggles,
Those within me,
Those of my own making,
And those I have inherited from the world.
Still, I listen to dreams
As I step through my sinful sludge to true transformation.
by Sr. Kathleen Nealon, CSR

So why the name X-Man? As inspired by my Pastor, Reverend Ronald O. Perry, "every man and woman in church has sinned, meaning we are all an X something." **X** is from the mathematical use meaning an unknown quantity or secret variable. See, your sins may be unknown to man, but are known and forgiven by God. **X** has also been used as an abbreviation for "Christ the anointed one", as in XMAS **(Christmas),** and Xianity **(Christianity).** So X-Man is synonymous with Christ-Man. Christ replaced our **X** with His cross, so we can be freed from the bondage of sin. The bible states we have all sinned and fallen short of God's glory. "If any man be in Christ, he is a new creature [X-Man]; old things are passed away; behold, all things have become new." *(2 Corinthians 5:17).* A real man in Christ is an X-Man a Christ-Man. It took me 36 years to realize I needed to become a member of the X-Men and join the ranks of David, Peter, Paul, Isaac, Jacob, Moses and other saved, sanctified full-of-the-Holy Ghost believers. An X-Man is a Christ-Man.

The goal of the Christian life is ". . . to be conformed to the image of His Son," *(Romans 8:29)*. When we are taught about the lives of Christian men most of the focus is put on their walk with the Lord with very little attention on the road traveled to get there. In other words more time is spent on their life's information rather than their life's transformation. How does one get from Sinner to Saint. How does one reach his ultimate goal TO BE MORE LIKE CHRIST. Paul wrote: "But we all, with unveiled face, beholding as in a mirror the glory of the Lord, are being transformed into the same image from glory to glory, just as by the Spirit of the Lord. *(2 Corinthians 3:18).*

The X-Man's life is one of transformation from glory to glory beholding the face of God. The word "transformed" comes from the Greek word metamorphoo (met-am-or-fo-o) which means "to change into another form, to transform, to transfigure." The word "metamorphosis" is derived from this word, which we use to describe the process of a caterpillar changing into a butterfly. It is also used to describe Jesus on the Mount of Transfiguration. *(Matthew 17: 1-2).*

When people hear the story of my evolution from Country Boy, to Attorney, to Author, to Minister, they begin to understand. And when they finally participate in one of my seminars or study sessions they state that the message is powerful. There now exists a church study group that teaches the transformation of men, a group where Men can shed their toughness and begin a process of becoming emotionally free, so that the little boy inside can finally grow up. "When I was a child, I spake as a child, I understood as a child: but when I became a man, I put away childish things" *(1 Corinthians 13:11)*. Transformation is for all Christians not just a select few! We are transforming into a new creature by beholding the face of God daily.

Before we begin studying our step-by-step process, let me first give you my testimony. I've been asked how I did it or how did I make it, as if *I* had anything to do with it. I confess it is by the grace and mercy of God, that I'm even alive today. As to the issue of how I made it, the fact is I have not made it. I am still transforming and evolving daily from one level of glory to another as I continue to behold the face of God. If it were not for the events of October 21, 2005, and the twelve days that followed, I would still be lying to myself that I had everything under control. One thing I know now is that I'm on a journey and my destination is Heaven. I confess that if it had not been for the Lord on my side, I do not know where I would be. When I was down, God would not count me out. When my enemies rose up against me, it was the Lord on my side. When the world wanted to swallow me up, God would not give me up. When I needed help my help was found in the Lord who made heaven and earth. It was God who reminded me why I was created in his image and gave me the strength to regroup, refocus and press forward toward my transformation and write this, the first of many X-Men books to come.

I've found my place in God-I'm an X-Man. However, I did not get here overnight and God is not finished with me yet. So every now and then throughout this book, I will pause to tell you a little about my conversion, confessions, testimony and transformation. I tell you about my evolution not just for your benefit and encouragement, but for my benefit as well. "But I keep under my body, and bring it into subjection: lest that by any means, when I have preached to others, I myself should be a castaway"(*1 Corinthians 9:27*). For 36 years I was sinking deep in sin far from the peaceful shore. I was buried deeply and stained within, sinking to rise no more. But as it happened to Peter, the Master of the sea heard my desperate cry and stretched out His hand into the water and lifted me. I tell you it was His love that lifted me, from a continuous sinful mutation **(moving further away from the image in which I was created)** and set me up for a heavenly transformation.

This transformation is progressive. It doesn't happen all at once, but gradually. As stated we are "being transformed (present tense), not "have been transformed" (past tense). Transformation involves a growth process. Transformation is not to be confused with Mutation-"The act or process of being altered or changed. In today's society, we are hooked on looks. Magazines and Television tell us how we're too fat, too tall, too skinny, too young, too old, too bald, too gray, or too hairy. In some shape, form or fashion we're not good enough. We have been made to believe that we don't measure up to society's view of perfection. Plastic surgery has become a multi-billion dollar industry. As consumers we indulge in every form, from cosmetic surgery, liposuction to silicone. People everyday are getting enhancements, augmentations, reductions, implants, lip sculpture, facelifts, eyelid surgery, etc. Anything about your exterior body that you don't like can be changed if you are willing to pay. However, no amount of money will pay for the internal transformation God will perform. God wants to change your behavior and spirit, and transform you into a new creature created in his image. X-Men God wants to alter your character, not your body.

Brother, you have been chosen by God to participate in his original reality show of transformation called the, "Extreme Makeover." Makeover is defined as an overall treatment to improve the appearance or change the image of something; A complete reconstruction and renovation. So what are the similarities or differences between X-Men mutants and X-Men for Christ? What makes your X-Man makeover extreme is the internal distinctions of your transformation. First, the comic book X-Men superheroes mutate. Mutation is a physical outward change. X-Men Christians are converted and transformed from the inside, spiritually. Secondly, X-Men-mutants, in order to learn to use their powers attend Xavier's School for Gifted Children whereas X-Men Christians are convicted by and filled with the Holy Spirit as they attend Sunday Schools, Bible Studies, Seminaries and Church. Third, the leader of the X-Men superheroes is Professor Xavier, whereas the leader for X-Men Christians is Christ. Fourth, X-Men mutants went to school so they could learn how to perfect their powers, how to use them without hurting themselves or others, so they could be used to fight evil, protect the innocent, save lives, save themselves to serve a greater purpose. X-Men Christians before God can use you he will send you to the "School of Life AKA Hard Knox" to prepare you with hope, humility faith and character to carry out your calling.

At my church in Beacon, Pastor Perry has structured our Mission statement as follows: "to win the lost and empower believers to be fully functioning followers of Christ". Springfield Baptist Church is a purpose driven Church. X-Men are driven men, recruiters of Men. The question, X-Men, is "what drives you?" I have come to understand that attitude drives actions. Actions drive results. Results drive lifestyles and accomplishments. If you are not happy with your results look at your actions and change your philosophy. Your attitude X-Men will determine your outcome and final transformation. Your attitude, will determine His attitude toward you on Judgment Day.

You have to be a real man to qualify as an X-Man. However, to be a real man one must understand what it means and does not mean. Man is defined as a human being created in God's image (Gen. 1:26), including male and female. To be created in God's image includes freedom of choice and responsibility for creation. Despite the biblical definition of man, I realize some men think that manhood means making children and providing for them, or simply attaining the age of 18 or 21. Manhood is not simply a matter of being male and reaching a certain age. These are acts of nature; manhood is a sustained act of character and responsibility. If the ability to reproduce were synonymous with manhood, than a rooster, like the one that crowed when Peter denied Christ, would be a better man than you or me. Rabbits reproduce every 40 days, but they are not men. Manhood cannot be measured by weight because an elephant weighs more than your entire family, nor by speed because a dog runs faster than you, nor by height because X-Men Giraffes are very tall, nor by cleverness, as a fox can be cleverer than you or me. X-Men show and exemplify the true meaning of manhood. X-Men are leaders with heart. X-Men have courage and depth and are passionate about their faith. X-Men don't hold grudges, they tell the truth, acknowledge mistakes, shoulder responsibility for their failures and others and share credit for success. X-Men show affection, decency and are sensitive and compassionate. Every man is characterized as a male, but not every male is an X-Man. When God talks about accepting your calling, He is talking about men not males. True manhood does not depend on age but rather on commitment. God is calling for real men. X-Men, are you committed to beholding the glory of the Lord?

X-Men are believers who are doing what they promised God and are a qualified representative of the Savior in whose image they have been made. X-Men are men who do not put business before prayer and family. A man who puts anything or anyone before their calling of God is neither a real man nor an X-Man. If you care for your living more than you care for Him who gives you life, you are not an X-Man. X-Men fear God and are not afraid to accept their role as men and leaders. X-Men are men with strong dispositions. X-Men do what is asked by God and abstains from doing what they should not. If you care for your gifts more than you do for He who gave the gift, you're not an X-Man. The mere fact that He granted you life should make you humble and determined to become and walk as an X-Man.

X-Men are instinctively driven by a desire to "matter" in the world, to make a difference. Becoming a "New Creature" does not happen accidentally but with intention and purpose. Abraham more than any other biblical character shows us the way to becoming a New Creature. Like many of us, he faced a situation in which he had to learn to live a new lifestyle after having been raised in a pagan culture. In *Genesis 12:1-3* God instructed Abraham to leave his home and promised him that he would be the father of many nations and make his name great. Abraham put all his faith and trust in this one, all-powerful God. Now if you get caught up in the information of Abraham's life rather than his transformation one would be led to believe he did everything right on this journey of his. When you study his transformation we learned that he lied, lost faith and he went places where he had no business going, and yet God blessed him. Can you begin to imagine what God will do for you, if you step out in faith and believe?

So what if you are short of these characteristics, what can you do to jump-start your transformation? If you think it is too late for you, Brother, it is not, (remember the thief on the cross who repented). If you think you have plenty of time, you don't (consider the thief on the other cross who ridiculed Jesus). If you think you are undeserving of grace and salvation, you are wrong (consider the release of Barabas). Every man or woman has the right to be an X-man. It doesn't matter what you have done in your past or what you are doing right now. When you genuinely repent, God forgives you and accepts you as His child and directs your path. It does not matter what your X is, for nothing is impossible for God. ". . . He who began a good work in you will carry it on to completion until the day of Christ Jesus (*Philippians 1:6*).

When you read and study the remaining sessions of this book and review the questions in the study guide remember God wants you to give your life some serious thought. He wants to complete the work He has begun in you by transforming your past and altering your destiny for service. Your past is a brief but necessary reflection, while your future is yet to be realized. As I stated earlier, sometimes your worst moment is a prelude to your best, as humility comes before Honor. I know you have stumbled and fallen. It is alright to fall but you cannot stay down. If you do life will pass you by and in Hell you will lift up your eyes. I know you have made a mess of things. Nevertheless, God can use you. He wants to challenge and encourage you and most of all He wants you to stop straddling the fence and make a decision. He wants you to choose this day who will serve. "Therefore, if anyone [Man or Woman] is in Christ, he is a new creature [X-Man]; old things have passed away; behold, all things have become new. Now all things are of God, who has reconciled us to Himself through Jesus Christ, and has given us the ministry of reconciliation" (*2 Corinthians 5:17-18*).

If you want to begin to change, if you are ready for your transformation to begin you need to repent, believe and confess that Jesus Christ is the Son of God, that He was crucified, buried and rose on the third day with all power in heaven and earth. Sounds easy? Well it is not. The journey doesn't end when we find God. Saying the words may be easy, but lining up with the word can be difficult. Salvation is a serious undertaking. Knowing what you are in for, gives you an idea of what you have to look forward to. You will have before you many sleepless nights and agonizing days of struggle and suffering, joy and pain, happiness and peace, trial and persecution, blood, sweat and tears, but keep your head up, keep your eyes on the prize, for there is victory in Christ. In the end you shall put on your robe and wear a crown. Paul said, "That if thou shalt confess with thy mouth the Lord Jesus, that God hath raised him from the dead, thou shalt be saved. For with the heart man believeth unto righteousness; and with the mouth confession is made unto salvation. For whosoever shall call upon the name of the Lord shall be saved" (*Romans 10:9-10 and 13*).

X-Men, going to church will not make you a Christian anymore than going to a garage makes you a mechanic. A suit does not make you a man. A dress with matching shoes, hat and purse, does not make you a woman. A uniform of the Arm Forces will not make you a soldier. In order for you to become an X-Man more is required than your looking the part and reciting some words of scripture. Just because the preacher pleaded and entreated you to come to the altar while the choir was singing "Come to Jesus" and you—being caught up in the emotion of the moment and ashamed of what you did last night-reluctantly came and recited a few symbolic words, that does not make you saved. Your statement of affirmation only began the conversion process. If you do no more, if you refuse or fall short on your journey, the words you spoke would have just been symbolic. Nothing is easier than saying words. Nothing is harder than living them day after day. First of all, what you believe in your heart you must confess with your mouth. Paul stated, you have to believe Christ died for your sins and rose again on the third day before you can sincerely confess. Put another way, the rock on which Jesus built the church was not Peter's confession, but the sincerity of a confessing Peter. Confessing what you believe, my Brother, is the rock bottom truth. Your confession must be made with sincerity. Sincerity means the quality or condition of being sincere; open and truthful; genuineness, honesty, freedom from duplicity; not deceitful or hypocritical. X-Men, when you confess, be sincere.

When you have become an X-Man and joined the evolution you begin a process. Evolution is a process in which something passes by degrees from different stages-to a more advanced or mature level. Once in Christ we are all new as we begin to transform from our old self to our new self. If you were a liar-now in Christ you are an X-Liar. If you were a thief-you are now an X-thief. If you were an adulterer-you have become an X-Adulterer. From alcoholic to X-Alcoholic. From Drug addict to X-addict. From Drug Dealer to X-dealer. From gambler-to Giver; From sinner to Saint; From lost to Saved, From fear to Faith, From disrespect to Discipleship; From divorce to Deliverance. From Persecutor-to Preacher. From gossiper to Confident

Counselor; From Victim to Victorious; and From dishonor to Honor. It does not matter your past you can be a part of the X-Man Team. Christ promised that He would throw your sins into the sea of forgetfulness, never to bring them up again. Every man and woman in church is an X-something. No matter the façade, sin, fear or interior blemish that has come to exist, Jesus says you are an X-Man, a new creature. Every man born of the womb is holy, said the Lord. When all else fails, know that you once were lost but now you are found, you were blind, but now you see.

You may be looking at your self now and feeling you cannot make it; or you may feel you already got things together. Maybe you have found yourself on skid row. You may be known as the person who never did anything right. You may feel unclean and rejected. Maybe your heart is filled with shame and remorse or you are simply scared and confused. Know that you don't have to persuade God to forgive you. We are all forgiven, every last one of us. His forgiveness is offered freely all we have to do is ask Him.

I began this book with my new transformation as an X-man: however the remaining sessions takes us back to see how after spending the past twelve years struggling with inner demons and running away from God I had my transformational Damascus road experience. On that day of October 21st, I got held up long enough for Jesus and me to get reintroduced and for me to finally realize how tired I had become from running. I had been running like Forest Gump when he woke up and realized Jenny was gone. I can hear Satan now, yelling "Run, Edward Run!" For twelve years I ran and everywhere I ran Jesus found me. Finally I was prepared to give up running and accept my calling into the ministry. I was still lost in sin and my sins had found me out. Before this day, I thought I was saved. I looked saved. I had the suit, the talk and the walk, but God knew I still had a past I was trying to hang on to and it wanted to hang on to me. God knew that despite my exterior cover, I was still unclean inside. *He knew the face of my spirit.* He knew I was still handcuffed to my past. I had believed I was broken and injured beyond repair. However, Jesus looked down on me with his compassion and mercy. When He looked at my broken will and spirit, He knew all was not lost. He called in his surgical team, (the same team He had at creation in Genesis): The Father, Son and Holy Ghost, and after They conferenced on my behalf, They came back with a unanimous decision. We can rebuild him; We can make him stronger, We can alter him, We can transform him, we can make him faster, bolder, We can create in him a clean heart and renew his mind and spirit. We can give him everlasting life. By the redeeming blood of Jesus Christ, he will be known as the "X-Man."

Now that you have a general idea of the term X-Man, let me properly introduce myself. Hi, I'm Edward Benson, the X-Man, and I'm here to recruit you to join the evolution. Underneath my exterior facade is a man who by the grace and power of Christ comes to recruit other sinners for Him who can save their souls, for Him, the only One who is able to destroy both soul and body (Matthew 10:28).

SESSION TWO

Is It Alright To Cry?

Big Boys Don't Cry!

Teardrops
When you cry upon a pillow,
Or tears fall down a cheek.
It's just emotions overflowing,
Not a sign of being weak.

We show emotions in different ways,
We can often loose control.
We cry of memories cherished,
The ones in my heart and soul.

So When I cry I'm not ashamed,
It's not a thing I try to hide.
Teardrops flow when I feel pain,
Why keep it bottled inside.
by Hope Smith

X-Men, it is reassuring to know that you cannot sincerely come into contact with Jesus and leave the same way you came. Concerning the Wise Men who saw the star and visited Jesus at his birth, the Apostle *Matthew* wrote in *2:12 of his Gospel*: "And being warned of God in a dream that they should not return to Herod, they departed into their own country **another way.**" The two key words in this scripture are "**another way**". Brothers in Christ, when you come into sincere face to face contact with Jesus, you cannot help but go home another way. Much has been preached about the three Kings of Persia's visit with Jesus. They have become Biblical celebrities; they are the topic of Headliners and Legends, even little children recognize them on sight. Growing up, the three always made all the Christmas plays and was often seen on numerous Hallmark Cards. However, I rarely hear a message about the return trip home. Have you ever wondered what the trip home was like?

What was their transforming experience with Jesus really like? What was so super natural that it would make them return home—different? Looking the same—but different. Dressed the same—but different. Transformed from the inside out. Can you imagine the excitement, the relief, the joy and peace they must have experienced? X-Men when you leave home with the intent of meeting Jesus, you will not go back to Herod—you won't go back in your sin. The good news is you can start today by X (ing) some things out of your life. Remember that when the lame man met Jesus, he went home another way. When the demon possessed man living in the graveyard met Jesus, he went home another way. When the ten lepers met Jesus, they went home cleansed. When blind Bartimethus met Jesus he went home seeing all the sights. When the woman with the issue of blood touched Jesus-she went home healed. When the damsel that was dead met Jesus, she went home alive. When the woman at the Well of Jacob met Jesus, she dropped her water pot and went back into the city a different person. When Mary Magdalene met Jesus, she became an X-prostitute. When Saul met Jesus, he went from Saul the persecutor to Paul the preacher. X-Men you cannot sincerely come in contact with Jesus and return home the same way. You should not be able to attend Church, Sunday school and Bible Study on a consistent basis and return home the same way you came.

Just like the creation of the world, everything does not happen all at once. Transformation and evolution to a new creature is a process. I know it may be hard for some to find their way home, through suicide bombers, wars and rumors of wars, witchcraft, devil worship and paganism. However, now you are ready to begin your transformation, just like the Wise Men who fled at God's command from the corruption and violence of Herod. It is now time to make a stand and break the shackles and unlock the handcuffs of sin. It is time to cry out in the name of Jesus and put the devil in his place. The course maybe difficult, the decision hard, yet learning how to cry out may be the most faithful decision of your life. Crying out means to call out loudly, shout to demand or require immediate action or remedy, proclaim or announce in public. The first and foremost thing X-Men must learn is how to cry and cry out with emotions. Emotions are complex reactions that engage our bodies and minds. It is an undisputed fact that men are stubborn. I should know, after all, I am one. Men are taught that they should be strong. Crying is considered a form of weakness that men have been taught from birth not to express. As men we are taught by society to suppress our feelings. A man is not considered a real man if he cannot suppress his emotions. Boys are socialized away from emotions, to never be forthcoming and honest about our most inner feelings. They get picked on by their peers and are even admonished by their mothers that, "big boys don't cry." A man is not considered a real man if he cannot suppress his emotions to maintain public status. Consequently, most men are raised to be tough not to wear our emotions on the sleeves.

My father did not raise me to be emotionally sensitive. People used to describe him as being as gentle as a kitten, but meaner than a black snake. He had taught us how to be tough. All my youth, he had operated an illegal nightclub and for three years while I was a teenager, I was the bouncer on Thursday, Saturday and Sunday nights. I had a front row seat to Brookhaven's version of Sodom and Gomorra. My father always kept at least one gun and one knife on him at all times, even when he came to Church. He was known to have used one or the other to settle certain disputes. It was routine for me to see someone get cut or shot on a weekly basis, and not necessarily by him. It was not unheard of for my sisters and brothers to see someone get killed on Saturday night or even on Sunday morning before going to Sunday School or Church or to be awakened in the middle of the night by the police.

I've read statistics about children growing up in the inner city and the fears they face. I've even watched the reality show "Growing up Gotti." Let me say this: Gotti has NOTHING on—"Growing up Benson." Rarely would a day go by that we did not witness injury, suffering and death. Forget the fearless Marvel comic character DareDevil; we had our own real life version of Hell's Kitchen. I missed many stray bullets and side stepped a couple of knives and punches while growing up. We experienced a traumatic event at least once a week. Yet, no one ever came to us to talk about each tragedy. No one was really concerned about our thoughts or helped us to understand why or offered us counselling on what we did to survive each day. We could not watch television and hear Oprah and Dr. Phil give us insight and direction. As I reflect on the past, I think a therapist would probably say something like we "suffered chronic exposure to aversive stimuli requiring intervention to repair cognitive emotional and physiological damage." In short, we all needed therapy. None of us really knew the innocence of childhood even though none of us ever really complained. I thank God that my mother and my Aunt Mary Jane saw that we went to church.

As a result of my upbringing, I did not comprehend how to get in touch with my feminine side. It is hard to be sensitive, supportive, receptive and emotional especially when you have spent your entire life being assertive, take-charge, action oriented and bottom-line. I would often not argue or raise my voice, because I was taught that to do so was to act based on emotion without the benefit of intellect. When you are sixteen working as a bouncer, the last thing you need to do is act emotionally. This behavior was constant in my life as a Lawyer, businessman, and husband and sometimes even as a father. I submit to you however, you cannot begin to address your past trials, difficulties, and spiritual struggles and embarrassing experiences without getting emotional. I hate to destroy the myth, but a man is human and humans have emotions. Jesus cried—so what's wrong with you? There is a time and a place to deal with emotions and that time is now. X-Men, you must learn to balance the things you say you are and not. Sometimes crying is the only thing that works. X-Men it is time to go beneath your rugged and guarded exterior and cry out to Jesus. If you cry out to God, He will hear and answer you.

Generally speaking, Women are different from men in that they have no problem expressing their emotions. Women have no problem crying out. I grew up believing that men are not allowed to show vulnerability. The only emotions fostered by society for men are anger, aggression and lust and were allowed to feel guilt and shame—but never fear. Even today some of these emotions and feelings are more "acceptable" than others. Society has become so twisted that men are confused about what it means to be masculine. Men are expected to hide their emotions because society dictates that it threatens our sense of manliness. However, just because you try to hide, does not mean the emotions do not exist. Even the most grown up men have a need to cry sometimes and not just at funerals of love ones. X-Men, whatever you are dealing with, you are neither alone nor are you without hope. I know sometimes you may ask yourself "so what's the use?" Why try or what difference will it make?

X-Men I don't know what your experience may be. However I do recall what mine was. I was busy being everything society wanted me to be. Yet, I was far from what God wanted me to be. I was Mr. Everything in High School and College. I was in all the right clubs and played all the right sports. I was active in the community and in my local church. I was elevated from Junior Deacon to Sunday School Teacher and as an adult even served as chairman of the Deacon Board. I attended Copiah-Lincoln Community College in Wesson, Mississippi and completed my undergraduate degree at Millsaps College in Jackson. I went to Law School at Mississippi College School of Law graduated in 1995 and became an Attorney. I invested in successful businesses, made some shady deals as well and learned to harden myself emotionally even more.

Nevertheless my accomplishments could not measure up to the level of my sins. Nothing I had done had taught me how to deal with or address my emotions. I was living on top of the world, living in sin and emotionally hard as a rock. My first marriage had yielded me three beautiful children, but due to my lack of emotions and pride I couldn't make the marriage work. I held things in until it almost killed me. Everyday I wore my public mask and hid the man that God so desperately wanted to let out. I was like Peter Parker hiding the fact that he was really Spider Man.

As a man of the world, I forgot I was human. I forgot that it was alright to show emotion. I forgot that it was alright to admit I was human and had real problems. I mean I had issues. But instead of relying on my faith to heal my lack of emotion, I hide for fear of the crowd. Unlike the woman with the issue of Blood, I didn't press the crowd to touch Jesus. This woman was awesome. Her story of hope and faith was so awesome that both the Gospels of *Matthew* and *Luke* wrote about the incident (see *Mathew 9:20-21* and *Luke 8:40-48*). She exemplified hope of wanting better times, to improve one's current condition with a focus on the future. She had desire, optimism, expectations, trust, confidence, aspiration, assurance and belief. She prayed for 12 years, but no answer came or healing occurred. Yet she never lost her faith. To the contrary her faith increased with her trial for she knew that all she had to do was touch Jesus' garment and she would be healed. Let me break it down for you, First she had a step of faith—she went to where she knew Jesus would be. Second, she believed in His power. Third, she acted on her belief. As an X-Man you need to act on what you believe. I encourage you to learn from this story of hope and faith. I know some of you have suffered for extended periods of time-pleading for answers, for relief, for healing, for a break through to no avail. Don't think because God has not answered your cry that He does not love you. *Sometimes God's greatest gifts can be unanswered prayers.* Maybe He is telling you like He told Paul when he prayed about the thorn in his side, that His "grace is sufficient."

X-Men if need be, learn from my mistakes or at least learn from your own. Do not forget the power of God and act on what you believe. I had forgotten that God had the ability to break me and re-make me. Living my way had cost me more than I was willing to pay and even though I wanted to put on the breaks and turn toward God completely, I could not forget my past: the allegations, the indiscretions, the lack of emotion, the unethical conduct, the dishonesty and deceit of practicing law. I could not forget the guilt and shame hidden in the recesses of my mind. I knew the world, especially the Brookhaven community would not let me forget it either, so I kept trying to make it in life according to the world's standards. I kept allowing the devil to haunt me with my past. After three years I contemplated returning to the practice of law, I had missed the thrill of victory of being the champion and hero. However, the shame and guilt of the past, coupled with my desire to spend more time with my children wouldn't allow me to return. I asked my daughters about practicing law again, they responded: "not if it means you want be able to spend time with me." With that, the decision was a no-brainer. It was probably the most emotional and rational decision I have ever made.

As discussed earlier, women have no problems expressing their emotions. But they sometime forget that the men in their lives need emotional support as well. It is without questions that a woman's inspiration improves a man's aspirations. Men are not like women. When men are looking for support and encouragement, they don't turn to their friends. They don't meet up at the Sunday evening Book club. They turn to the woman in their lives: to their wife, their girlfriend or their mother. There are some men who believe that their inability to show emotion coupled with the lack of support from the women in their lives some how is justification for not being good husbands, why they are not going to church, and not being saved and active in Church. Additionally there are those who claim that these emotional difficulties have contributed to alcohol or substance abuse, violence or behavioral linked domestic violence. Like me, most men believe that society will not let them forget the past. Although the Church is full of Kingdom Cops (people who believe they have the right to judge and condemn), understand that God will not accept any of these man-made excuses on Judgment Day.

Brothers, I know you are constantly confronted with the pressures, pain, shame, humiliation and stress of past mistakes. Thus, you may have a tendency to become hard without emotion. I know despite having experienced heart-rendering pain you are expected to be tough, stoic, independent, demanding and aggressive without any thought about the nurturing aspects of masculinity. The world tells you not to be a sissy or punk, not to whine or be too sensitive. Rather than let go and let God, most men find it easier to conform to established standards and maintain the façade of living life on the World's terms. So what if you have felt a loss of power, identity, self-worth and purpose? I understand if you feel despondent, weak, helpless, hopeless and confused. X-Men, empower yourself by finding your rightful place in God, the Church and Society. If you don't cry, express valid emotions, or communicate, it makes it easier for you to slip into other sins.

Men of God, it is imperative that the women in your lives begin to understand you, thus enhancing the quality of your relationship. However, understanding you does not mean they should have to excuse, explain or justify your behavior. These Women will need your assistance as well. They need to know that you need and want a helpmate. They need to know that God created them just for you and for that alone you are grateful and satisfied. Women, your men will need your assistance as they pursue their destiny as X-Men. Your men will need to know that they can rise above their past sins, even from separation, divorce or incarceration. Even if you disagree with his decisions, he needs you to show him respect both publicly and privately, and pray for him daily. He does not need you to be like the wife of Job. Job's wife was his cheerleader and helpmate when things were going well, but she told Job to curse God and die when things were not. Women your men need you to be dedicated to them and to their vision. They need you to stand by him the whole way and never allow him to doubt their calling or God. They will need assurance to face their feelings in the context of Christ's love and forgiveness. They need to hear that every man (even he) can be resurrected and renewed in Christ.

SESSION THREE

A Time To Die

"If you haven't found something to die for, you are not fit to live."

X-Men if you have cried out and are ready to start your life's work-then it's time for you to die. It is time for you to dig a grave and bury some stuff. You cannot get to heaven without burying something in the graveyard of life. *Isaiah 55:6-8* states: "Seek ye the Lord while he may be found, call ye upon him while he is near: Let the wicked forsake his ways, and the unrighteous man his thoughts: and let him return unto the Lord, and he will have mercy upon him; and to our God, for he will abundantly pardon. For my thoughts are not your thoughts, neither are your ways, saith the Lord." God is waiting on you. He is standing at the door of your heart, knocking. Don't you think it is time you let Him in? You will never know how far God is prepared to take you, until you surrender and trust Him. Know this, at anytime you can leave your present life behind and start the race and fight for your eternal soul. Wherever you are right now is the perfect place to begin your journey to becoming an X-Man.

I know it is sometimes hard to shake off the influence of one's surroundings. However, if you are still dealing with some issues, I employ you to ask God to help you die to them. If you don't, those same influences will carry you straight to hell. If you are a gambler-die to gambling. If you are a gang banger-die to it. If you are a thief-die to stealing. If you are a liar-die to lying. If you are gay-die to homosexuality. If you are a fornicator-die to it. If you are a child molester, shady politician, spouse abuser, a pimp-die, spiteful and vindictive, a whore, tramp, slut or prostitute, dishonest and deceitful-just die to it all. If you desire a relationship with and be used by God, there are some things you are going to have to die to. When Jesus died for your sins and mine, He purchased us for a price. Thus, our first love should be for the man who paid the ultimate price for our salvation. X-Men are you willing and prepared to deny yourselves and die to the world for eternal life in Christ?

Jesus died for us all, for we have all sinned and fallen short of his glory. Just like the two thieves on Calvary we all have equal access to His glory. "And that He died for all, that they which live should not henceforth live unto themselves, but unto Him which died for them, and rose again. Wherefore, henceforth know we no man after the flesh: yea though we have known Christ after the flesh, yet now henceforth know we Him no more. Therefore, if any man be in Christ, he is a new creature: old things are passed away; behold all things are become new." *2 Corinthians 5:15-17.* It took Calvary for one of the thieves to repent and separate himself from his sinful nature. In order for you to become a new creature you will have to separate yourself from your past.

To understand your X-Man transformation, you must truly understand death for it is a relevant fact of life. There are three types of death. First is a spiritual death, which is the separation of the soul from God, a condition we inherited thanks to Adam (see *Ephesians 2:1, 5).* A second form of death is a physical death which is the separation of the soul from the body (see *Romans 5:12-14).* Finally, the third death occurs immediately after Judgment for a sinful life, an eternal death. The bible states: that it is appointed unto man once to die (physically), then the Judgment. An eternal death is the culmination and extension of spiritual death, the eternal separation of the soul from God in the lake of fire *(Revelation 20:14).* Understanding death is knowing that each breath you take could be your last.

For a person or something to die means to pass from an animate to a lifeless state; to cease to live; to suffer a total and irreparable loss of action of the vital functions; to become dead; to expire; to perish, depart or vanish. In order to keep yourself from experiencing a spiritual and eternal death, there are some natural people, places, things and habits that you will need to vanish, expire and perish from your life. I employ you to die to anything that separates your soul from God. God wants you to be separate, just like He separated the day from the night at creation. "Wherefore come out from among them, and be ye separate, saith the Lord, and touch not the unclean thing; and I will receive you" *(2 Corinthians 6:17).* It is time for the X-Man in you to come out and for your old nature to die.

We all know of someone who has died a physical death, but have you ever considered what will happen on the day you die? What will happen when you finally take your last breath? The doctor or coroner will pronounce you dead. The funeral home will come and get your body. Your family will make arrangements for a final service before your burial. Someone will probably read a scripture and say a prayer, the choir will sing a song and the minister will say a few words of encouragement. Obviously, the words of encouragement will not be for your benefit, because, after all, you're dead. Your opportunity to hear and receive the word would have come and passed. After the Minster is done, the funeral directors will take your body and **place** it in a hole in the ground called a grave plot and return you to the dirt from whence you came. Your family and friends will be taken somewhere to eat and fellowship while discussing truthfully how good or how bad you were. They will divide your belongings like the soldiers divided Jesus' clothes and then they will leave and go on with their lives only to reflect on their memory of you every now and then. Your life will only be remembered in their minds and on your tombstone or grave marker, if any. "For the living know that they shall die: but the dead know not any thing, neither have they any more reward; for the memory of them is forgotten" (*Ecclesiastes 9:5*). Your spirit will appear before Judgment to explain or justify your life on earth. Can you even begin to think what you will say to Jesus? What will your legacy be? What will your epitaph read? Can you even imagine spiritually attending your own funeral and viewing your dead corpse in the coffin and realizing how much time you wasted doing things your way?

There is an interesting show that comes on ESPN called "Beyond the Glory". Have you ever wondered what your life will be like after the glory of this life? What your life will be like if you do not make in to God's Glory? I attended a funeral back in 1993 of a long time deacon at one of the largest African American Churches in Brookhaven. The deceased had served as Deacon for over forty years. Attending his funeral were all of the local elected officials, his former co-workers, church family and four generations of heirs. The Minister who delivered his eulogy gave directives to the family members sitting on the first five pews. He stated: "if you're undecided whom you should grow up to be like, be like your grandfather". Obviously, the Minister believed the deceased to have been a great servant of God who provided for his family and worked diligently for his church and was well respected in the community. I knew of the gentleman and always respected him. The problem I had then and have now is why the heirs couldn't be encouraged to be like Christ. Even though the deceased was believed to have been a good man, no indication was given about his salvation. X-Men it is not enough for you to simply be a good man or woman: you need to be a saved man or woman. If you are to survive an eternal death, the fact that you've been working in the church faithfully for 40 years alone will not do it. If you're not saved when you meet your physical death, you are going to catch Hell when you see Jesus.

X-Men, what are you willing to die for? Are you willing to die for your family and country? Are you willing to die for Christ? Today, as you begin to analyze your life in all aspects, pray with persistence that old things are passed away, and let nothing separate you from the love of Jesus Christ. It does not matter where this book has found you; what matters is what you do with the information and guidance that God will give you as you study. X-Men, I challenge and beseech you not to receive the grace of God in vain. God has heard your heart's cry for salvation and has stated that this is the time of acceptance and the day of salvation. "But in all things approving ourselves as ministers of God, in much patience, in afflictions, in necessities, in distresses, In stripes, in imprisonments, in tumults, in labors, in watching, in fasting; By pureness, by knowledge, by longsuffering, by kindness, by the holy ghost, by love unfeigned, by the word of truth, by the power of God, by the Armor of righteousness on the right hand and on the left, by honor and dishonor, by evil report, and good report: as deceivers and yet true; As unknown, and yet well known; as dying and behold, we live; as chastened, and not killed; As sorrowful, yet always rejoicing; as poor, yet making many rich; as having nothing, and yet possessing all things (*2 Corinthians 6:5-10*). As an X-Man, you possess everything you need to walk in the anointed calling God has for your life. However, as a part of your transformation, you are required to die to your sins.

John 3:16 states; "For God so loved the world, that He gave His only begotten Son, that whosoever believe in Him should not perish, but have everlasting life." When Jesus was in the garden of Gethsemane looking into the cup, praying that the cup would pass Him by, it was you, your face He saw inside the cup that is why He endured the cross. In order for you to live as an X-Man you will have to endure and die. In order for you to receive everlasting life, you will have to die (separate yourself from some stuff) before you Die. *Luke 9:23* states: "And He said to them all, If any man will come after Me, let him deny himself, and take up His cross daily, and follow Me. For whosoever will save his life shall lose it: but whosoever will lose his life for My sake, the same shall save it." X-Men, it is time for you to walk through the valley and shadow of death and fear no evil, for God will be with you and He alone will comfort you.

2 Corinthians 4:8-12 states: "We are troubled on every side, yet not distressed; we are perplexed, but not in despair; Persecuted, but not forsaken; cast down, but not destroyed; Always bearing about in the body the dying of the Lord Jesus, that the life also of Jesus might be made manifest in our body. For we which live are always delivered unto death for Jesus' sake, that the life also of Jesus might be made manifest in our mortal flesh." X-Men must die to sin in order to walk in life with Christ. Are you surrounded by trouble? Are you distressed, perplexed, depressed and despaired? Do you sometimes feel forsaken and cast down? Don't fret, my brother, for you will not be destroyed. Keep hoping, praying and trusting God. *Romans 6:4 & 6* states: "Therefore, we are buried with Him by baptism into death; that like as Christ was raised up from the dead by the glory of the Father, even so we also should walk in newness of life. Knowing this, that our old man is crucified with Him, that the body of sin might be destroyed, that henceforth we should not serve sin." X-Men don't you want a new life? Are you not tired of serving Satan and sin? Don't you know that no matter how much wealth you accumulate in this life, no matter what your accomplishments the wages of sin is still death (*Romans 6:23*).

You are an X-Man, a new anointed creature of God. God has forgiven your sins. He has been patient with you. If you were sincere with your repentance, He has brought you out of whatever sin you were trapped in and now you work for Him. The question my friend is now that you know Him-will you trust Him? As a man of God, it does not matter how you started out, what matters is how you finish the race. Yes, contrary to popular opinion, you have the opportunity to write your conclusion in life. When Jesus hung His head on Calvary, He stated it is finish. X-Men it was finished just for you. He finished it so you would have no excuse not to run the race set before you.

Some may think that you may have gone too far or have sunk too deep into sin and it will take you forever to get back home into the loving arms of Christ our Savior. I once read a story about a salesperson traveling down a rural road. Feeling lost, he spotted a girl of about 12-years-old by the roadside and he asked her, "How far is it to the Robinson Farm?" "Well sir," said the bright young lady, "it's about 24,996 miles the way you are heading now. But if you turn around and go the other way, it will only take about three miles." X-Men, sometimes all it takes is a change in directions. The thought of traveling down a road of destruction not knowing which exit to take to travel a different road, is almost unbearable. Nevertheless, I submit that your spiritual travel away from God is like taking a trip for the first time, uncertain whether you will get lost on the way or exactly how long it will take you to get to your destination. However, when you are on your way back home, the trip does not take long at all. You always get back faster than the time it took to take the journey. That is the way of our spiritual journey is with Christ. The thief on the Cross-spent a lifetime traveling the road that lead him to Calvary, but it only took a few moments to get directions to Paradise. Your return trip to get back to Christ is instant; it does not take hours, days, weeks or even years. You don't have to go on Map Quest, Yahoo or Goggle for directions. Just pull into your Biblical Service Station and ask the attendant, "How do I get to Heaven from here?" The response is: "All you have to do is surrender, believe and repent." It is time to quit dying spiritually by traveling the road of sin and destruction, farther away from God. It is time for X-Men to comeback home, to exit the highway of destruction and get on the highway to heaven. By the way, once you change directions get in the fast lane and don't worry about the speed limit or about getting a ticket. Your heavenly Father left a deposit on Calvary that will cover the cost of all your tickets and fines.

You may have lived a secret life that only you and God know about, but now is the time to die to it. Whatever mess you have made of your allegedly miserable and unfulfilled life, its time for you to die to it. "Jesus answered him (Peter) with thou lay down thy life for my sake? Verily, verily, I say unto thee, the cock shall not crow, till thou hast denied me thrice (*John 13:38*). Peter was later convicted not by words, but by the crow of a rooster. What will it take for God to convict you? How many times in your life have you denied Christ? If you want your ways to line up with God's there are some things you are going to have to die to. If you don't know how to die, ask God. X-Men and X-Women, again I say this: you will need to die before you Die. "It is a faithful saying: For if we be dead with Him, we shall also live with Him: If we suffer, we shall also reign with Him: if we deny Him, He also will deny us (*2 Timothy 2:11-12*).

X-Men the more you deny and die to self, the stronger your relationship with Christ will be. Your faith will allow you to move mountains, divide seas and be forgiven. But you must die to your hatred and unforgiveness, if you expect God to forgive you. Is there someone in your life you need to forgive? Have you died to the hatred you have for your enemies? X-Men, if you still need help dying, just ask God. But die before you Die. Ask, and it shall be given you; seek, and ye shall find; knock, and it shall be opened unto you: [8] For everyone that asketh receiveth; and he that seeketh findeth; and to him that knocketh it shall be opened (*Matthew 7:7-8*). Why don't you just die already so you can go home another way?

There is another story about a young girl who rode the school bus everyday to school. Everyday the bus driver would pick her up and drop her off in front of her house. One day she noticed that the bus driver did not drop off one little boy in front of his house. Instead, this little boy got dropped off in front of the graveyard. After the bus driver had dropped the little boy off, the little girl asked, "why is it that you drop me and everybody else on the bus off at our homes, but you drop off this boy in front of the graveyard?" After a degree of hesitation, the bus driver responded, "you see, little girl, this boy lives on the other side of the graveyard and the bus is unable to travel down his narrow street, thus in order for him to get home, he has to go through the grave yard." In order for any of us to get home at the end of life's journey, we must go through the graveyard. X-Men, in order for you to get to heaven you will have to go through the graveyard of your life. Nobody else can do it but you. As much as I love you as a person, I cannot go through it for you. It is a personal decision, its' your personal choice, for we all have many graves to dig and sins to bury.

If you haven't arrived yet and still are living in your sin, do not be discouraged, Christ came to save the lost. He came to save you and me. God does not care how you come to Him; all He cares about is that you have come to Him. It doesn't matter where you are, if you put yourself there or if God put you there. I implore you to hear the warnings of God. You do not have forever; you may not even have the next hour. Time is not a luxury to be taken for granted. I had a nephew who died at age eleven. When I think about the fact that I could have died in my eleventh year of running from God, I cannot help but shout about God's grace. I could have died in my sins and my eternity would have been spent in hell. X-Men don't think you have forever to come home. X-Men don't think you have to clean up your life before you come home. The prodigal son, when he came home after losing all he had was a miserable failure and a disgrace to everyone but not to his father. His father opened up his arms wide in unconditional love and acceptance. Notice the scripture doesn't say he cleaned himself up and tried to appear as something he wasn't. He didn't try to cover up his sins with fig leaves. He didn't blame his friends he left back in the city. He simply came home (*John 11:43-44*) and "Brethren, I count not myself to have apprehended: but this one thing I do, forgetting those things which are behind, and reaching forth unto those things which are before, I press toward the mark for the prize of the high calling of God in Christ Jesus" (*Philippians 3:13-14*). It is time to forget your past and press toward Jesus. It's time to press through the crowd, climb the highest tree and scream at the top of your voice, "Master, can you use me?"

SESSION FOUR

Master Can You Use Me?

"So what if you've broken all Ten Commandments?"

X-Men, now that you have died to your sin and become reborn, God want to use you. On the front cover of this book it reads: "Lord you said you could use anyone, But can you use me?" The key word is "But." But, means that there is an issue of concern, a degree of uncertainty. I knew my sins, just like you know yours. I was aware of my shortcomings, just like you are aware of yours. I believed God knew my every thought, just like He knows yours. Yet, when I first wanted to give my life totally and completely to God, I was concerned if He could really sincerely and truthfully use someone as sinful as me. All I could think about was "God You don't know all of my sins. You don't know about all the lies. You don't know about the people I've caused to suffer or the hurt and pain I've caused". I was so focused on my personal inadequacies, that I could not see Christ. All I knew was that I did not desire to be found dead without Him in my life.

My brother, R. W. Benson, Jr., was a good example of and an inspiration for someone changing their lifestyle by becoming born again. I recall when he died in October 1999. It was the first death of a sibling I had experienced. I had just acquired a financial interest in a new funeral home and the first person buried there was my brother. Although he died of a massive heart attack, he had lived a homosexual lifestyle all of his adult life. He would often dress up like a woman and had lived with numerous male partners in Baton Rouge, Louisiana. Despite our home life, we had both been raised in the Church and had even sung in the choir together doing our teenage years. We both knew what was right and what was wrong. We would often hear preachers joke about how God had made Adam and Eve and not Adam and Steve. Yet, growing up, no one ever had any serious talks with us regarding boyhood to manhood or gave us advice on male sexuality. Because of our difference of opinion in lifestyles, we did not spend much time with each other. I was ashamed of him and his life style and allowed it to some degree keep us apart. However, when he died, I begin to question myself in a self-examination. Who was I to judge his lifestyle or behavior? Who was I but a sinner? I was breaking every commandment and then some, yet I had the audacity to look down on my brother.

I should have been praying for his deliverance. I should have been repenting and cleaning up my own life. When I got the telephone call that my brother had died, all I could think about was the opportunities I had missed to tell him how much I loved him. The times I could have driven to Baton Rouge and spent the weekend and simply just fellowshipped with my brother. God accepts us all just as we are. Who was I to play Kingdom Cop?

The most peculiar thing about my brother's death, even in my sinful state, is that I was concerned about his soul. Even though there was nothing I could do, I found myself wondering if he had ever gotten his life right with God. It is quite something to be so removed from a person's life that you don't know if they ever had a righteous relationship with Christ. You should have seen me when his Pastor spoke at his funeral in Brookhaven. It was heart—lifting when he shared with our family how just two weeks earlier at his church in Louisiana, my brother had come to the altar to confess and sincerely repent of his sins, shouted (cried out) before the church. He was back in the church witnessing to people to make a change. I became full of joy to know that my brother had died and had been "Born Again" before he Died.

Even after learning of my brother's salvation it was not sufficient for me to give God my life. It wasn't enough for me to give up my worldly life and die. It took me six more years. Six years that I had no idea of knowing that I would actually see. Six years of reading obituaries and being ungrateful that my name was not in print. Six years that I was not entitled to, but granted by grace. I don't know, but maybe like me you are looking over your past with great remorse that says, "if I could go back and do it all over again, I wouldn't do it or I would do things differently". If only life had a rewind button. I wish I could go back and change it, but I cannot. I wish I could tell my brother I'm sorry and beg for his forgiveness. I am finally in tune with my emotions and sometimes I even cry. When I look over my past, like David, I can encourage myself without seeking anyone's approval. No other person was there when the Lord brought me out. X-Men, it should not matter if your family understands your praise-worship. They may never truly know what God has brought you through. No one will or should appreciate God's grace and mercy in your life more than you. You will never fully know my evolution process and I will never truly know yours. I just pray that you evolve before you die. Just in case you are wondering if the Master can use you, I come with assurance that He can. You simply have to want to be used.

Even if you've broken all Ten Commandments, God can still use you. Our God can take a drug user and make him an Usher. He can take a pimp and make him a preacher. In fact it is your past that qualifies you for present service. God has a job opening and He has reviewed your resume, with the hope that you will come in for an interview. Your end has not come. God wants to use you. There are numerous ways you can turn your sin into a blessing for others. He is using me by writing this book to tell my story to reach others, to accept His calling into ministry. You may be called to Preach, Tithe, Teach a Bible Class, Outreach, Mission trips, Youth field trips, join the praise team, drama ministry, become a Deacon, Deaconess, Trustee, Choir member, attend or organize a conference or seminar, evangelism in your community, start a Crusade, serve as Servant Leader, visit a Nursing Home, visit/call and pray for the sick, work with Christian Radio or Television. I can't even begin to touch the surface of the various ways you can lift up the Kingdom of God by changing lives, one person at a time. As you continue to die as you walk in your calling, consider how many lives are touched each day by your ideas of Christ. ***Brothers life is too short for pity parties. Get busy living, or get busy dying.***

X-Men is there something about your life that you feel ashamed of that's keeping you from your calling? Are you being hindered by your shortcomings or lack of self-identity. Is there someone in your family of whose life style you are ashamed of? "I speak to your shame. Is it so that there is not a wise man among you? No, not one that shall be able to judge between his brethren? But brother goeth to law with brother and that before the unbelievers. Now therefore there is utterly a fault among you, because ye go to law one with another. Why do ye rather take wrong? Why do ye not rather suffer yourselves to be defrauded? Nay, ye do wrong, and defraud, and that your brethren. Know ye not that the unrighteous shall not inherit the kingdom of God? Be not deceived: neither fornicators, nor idolaters, nor adulterers, nor effeminate, nor abusers of themselves with mankind, Nor thieves, nor covetous, nor drunkards, nor revilers, nor extortioners, shall inherit the kingdom of God. And such were some of you: but ye (X-Men) are washed, but ye (X-Men) are sanctified, but ye (X-Men) are justified in the name of the Lord Jesus, and by the spirit of our God" (*1 Corinthians 6:5-11*). Knowing what you know about your life, you should come running to the altar screaming, "Master can you use me?" You should come crashing through the brick wall of your sins, ready to fly into action as an X-Man. ***Make peace with your past so it won't screw up the present.***

"Then said I, Woe is me! For I am undone; because I am a man of unclean lips, and I dwell in the midst of a people of unclean lips: for mine eyes have seen the King, the Lord of hosts. Then flew one of the seraphims unto me, having a live coal in his hand, which he had taken with the tongs from off the alter: And he laid it upon my mouth, and said, Lo, this hath touched thy lips: and thine iniquities is taken away, and thy sin purged. Also I heard the voice of Lord, saying, Whom shall I send, and who will go for us? Then said I, Here am I; send me" (*Isaiah 6:5-8*). Each of us are granted numerous opportunities to experience God's love for ourselves. We all have free will to be used of God. Choose this day whom you will serve. If you genuinely desire to know the bliss, prosperity, joy, divine presence and peace that only comes from having trust, faith and the love of God then it is time for God to use you.

The Pharisees brought a woman caught in adultery to Jesus demanding that He follow the law of Moses-that she should be stoned. They wanted to kill her. However, Jesus responded, "He who is without sin let him cast the first stone." Slowly each man walked away. Jesus asked the woman, "where are your accusers?" Jesus told her to go and sin no more. X-Men, when Jesus wants you to die to something, He tells you to go and sin no more. Usually the most unqualified people will want to condemn you, but Jesus simply says to go and sin no more. For Christ the scars of your sins are not permanent. His grace is greater than your past. In *Isaiah 43:18-19* the Lord stated: "Remember ye not the former things, neither consider the things of old. Behold, I will do a new thing; now it shall spring forth, shall ye not know it? I will even make a way in the wilderness, and rivers in the desert." In short if you let him, God will make a way out of no way. He will allow you to bury your past in the graveyard; in fact He will supply the shovel. If you are sincere with your repentance He will say, "Go and sin no more." Once you decide to separate yourself from your sinful nature, God can use you.

Even Moses was used despite a sinful past. "And Moses said unto God, Who am I, that I should go unto Pharaoh, and that I should bring forth the children of Israel out of Egypt?" *(Exodus 3:11)*. Moses knew his past and he knew the Egyptians and the Hebrews back in Egypt knew his past as well. They knew he had committed murder and buried the Egyptian in the sand. Moses even made excuses. I can imagine him saying, "the people wont believe me and I'm not a great speaker, although he had no problems talking to Pharaoh when he lived with him. I can imagine Moses said who am I to accept this calling. Who am I to deliver these people? Who am I, that I should go back to Pharaoh. Who am I, if not unqualified? Who am I, if not unjustified?" Nevertheless, despite his past, God anointed Moses as deliverer of Israel and told him; "certainly I will be with thee." If the Lord could use a basket case like Moses and other people like Peter, Paul and even me, then certainly he can use you. Nehemiah rebuilt the walls of Jerusalem, while his name was being mocked and slandered. Abraham, a known liar was blessed with a son and a nation. Noah had problems with alcohol, but he built the Ark. X-Men, God can use you. Jacob was a liar and a trickster, Gideon was afraid, Samson was a womanizer, Jeremiah and Timothy were too young, Elijah was suicidal, Barabass was a terrorist and Lazarus was dead. It is because of our past that God wants to use us. Had it not been for their past, these guys would not have had a future.

Let us back up a bit. God spoke to Abraham personally, actually visited him in his home, and even considered him a friend. Abraham loved God and was even willing to sacrifice his son to prove his faith. I have often heard Abraham and other Old and New Testament men described as if they were some form of biblical superheroes, kind of like the Three Wise Men and Three Hebrew Boys. I agree they get preached about as if they themselves were superhuman. But each of them, like the rest of us, has and had many shortcomings and weaknesses. In each biblical hero's life there were obvious test and trials, successes and failures, ups and downs, moments of worry, doubt, indecision and frustration. Their journey to stardom is just like an X-Man's transformation: a journey with a starting point, a route and a destination toward eternal life.

In a Bible of Big Names, our true heroes tend to be anonymous, the unheard of and overlooked often living in the shadows. Habakkuk and Obadiah have entire Old Testament Books named after them, but you rarely hear their names mentioned on Sunday morning or Wednesday night Bible Study. True heroes are not well known like in today's society. We call them the unsung heroes, like teachers, nurses, the firemen, policemen and rescue workers who sacrificed their lives during the 9-11 attacks on the World Trade Centers in New York City. Mason Cooley stated, "Necessity makes heroes of us all." Those who are often underpaid, unidentified, no tapered parade, the team player, the silent helper, like my man HUR who held up the hands of Moses at Rephidim with Aaron (*See Exodus 17:10-12*). HUR may not have been one of the Biblical Big names. He would not be considered a Sunday Morning Headliner or Legend, but what a Hero he was. Necessity of the Israelites winning the battle was contingent on Moses' arms not growing weary. This caused for heroic humility, sacrifice, courage and boldness on behalf of HUR and he did it without any regard for recognition.

X-Men like HUR, you do not have to wear a cape or a pair of tights to be a hero. You do not have to come flying through the clouds to save the day. You may not get the recognition you deserve, but when you allow God to use you, you become a Hero. We have been taught to believe that Superheroes are fictional characters with some extraordinary or superhuman powers. Our X-Men heroes represent courage, strength, humility and advance a greater good by going beyond normal expectations of goodness and bravery. X-Men are not fictional characters like the Hulk. X-Men Christian heroes are real people, who have battled their inner demons in a daily fight to control the raging sin within. When I am asked who I am, I reply, "I am X-Man, a newly anointed creature, who by the grace and power of Christ (my Superpower within) has been transformed and now comes to recruit other sinners for Him who can save their souls." God is calling you to come to repentance before you Die. He is pleading your cause that you will live, grow, and persevere in faith until the end. Don't make excuses, join the evolution. My God wants to use you!

SESSION FIVE

Who Are You Trying To Impress?

"Dress to Impress"

When you are ready to be used by God, you will not have to worry about impressing the crowd. We are a society that competes for attention to the extent that our appearance is a major preoccupation, even an obsession. At the Grammies and the Oscars, there is more talk about the dresses and hairstyles worn by the actors and actresses being recognized than about their actual work. I know as men, we are often working on our game, making sure we are able to still impress the ladies, especially if we are meeting them for the first time. Men feel a powerful drive to impress and avoid rejection or failure. A man is on his best behavior as he tries to figure out what to say to get a woman's attention. He does not want to offend her or scare her off. He wants to impress her. Since the Million Man March we have stopped educating our young men and the Church no longer actively takes charge. Our young men are taking their cues from M-T-V, B-E-T and R or X-rated movies. Today our young men have their favorite rap songs to educate them how on how to be men and how to relate to women. They learn first-hand how to be derogatory, insulting or otherwise disrespectful.

It probably sounds incredible. Even I tried to impress a few girls in the past. I know I was trying to impress Aisha when we first met. I wanted her to like me and be pleased with me. I wanted her to think I was something special. So I listed my accomplishments and successes back in Brookhaven (I certainly didn't share my failures there). In fact my actions almost turned her off. It wasn't until a later telephone call that she got to see the real me and decided she actually liked me. Aisha and I both share two friends who dated for four months and fell in love without ever having met each other. She was living in New York and he was in the Air force stationed in Afghanistan. They had only communicated via e-mail and telephone and yet, after years of searching for that perfect match and moving from bad to decent relationships, they found love ordained by God. Now, whatever they were expressing to each other in their communication, had to have been impressive!

I am certain whether you are a man or woman reading this book, that you can recall a few times when you wanted to impress someone. Whether you are going to a job interview, in public speaking or simply dressing up, you want to impress. Why do we dress to impress? Why do we have to wear the right clothes for job interviews? Why is there a difference between your everyday clothes and your Church clothes? Does God not see you the other days of the week? Why is it so important to prepare when making a presentation, to put our best foot forward when meeting someone new. X-Men in your pursuit to impress, be careful not to impress the wrong people. Do not impress for the wrong reasons, for example, to get the ladies and do not go over board or be dishonest to cover up your faults or to make yourself out to be more of a man than you are. In college, I knew a guy, who loved to impress the girls. His favorite statement was, "I'm 285 pounds of frustration and aggravation, men, women and children look at me in amazement and disbelief. You're looking at the only man who can talk sugar to a woman and make her cry syrup." Most of the time instead of impressing, we only make ourselves look stupid.

When you try to impress, worrying about appearances, it deters you from dealing with the inside. You lose focus and you only cover up what needs the most work. Did you know that while most of your jobs and relationships were built on personal achievement, all God wants from you is faithfulness and obedience? You don't have to make an impression on God; God wants to make an impression on you. You don't have to play the blame game, even though you may strive daily to die to the world, know that none of us are perfect. So when you mess up you don't have to prejudge God—like Adam. Adam had dominion over everything and the first time he failed he wanted to hide from God. Adam hid because he assumed God wouldn't understand. X-Men don't assume that God will not understand when you have made a mess of things. After all, God made you, so don't hide from Him. Don't go get some fig leaves and try to dress to impress to cover up your mess. Don't cover your faults with fluff and lies. Be real, honest and open, which will invite the right people into your sphere. Just be yourself! Don't let your attempt to impress be viewed as insecurity. Don't be insecure because you have a past. Insecurity leads to nervousness which leads to anxiety, which leads to low self-esteem which ultimately is rooted in the fear of not measuring up or of doing something embarrassing. You cannot be an X-Man if you hide from the people you have hurt. I understand that some of you may feel lost and confused, or angry and alienated and social adjustment may seem impossible. You have been lead to believe that you cannot live down an accusation of child abuse, a drug conviction, being HIV positive, domestic violence, conviction and incarceration. In this age of war against terrorism it is hard for some to live a normal life because they come from the wrong ethic group, wear the wrong clothes or have the wrong skin color. I remember a time when only African Americans had a skin tone problem. Nevertheless, God said He is faithful and just to forgive. God accepts us not because of our skin tone or because our spirits are unblemished but because he knows our weakness and He is able to restore us. Now, how impressive is that?

If you are not pre-occupied with impressing others, you will not have to be afraid. Adam confessed to God "I was afraid." Like Adam, we sometimes want to point the finger, "she made me do it." Are you making excuses for your sins? When you sin against God, whom do you blame? Are you like Adam, afraid of God? Are you afraid you will be rejected? God chose you because He knows your heart. Nothing about you is hidden from God's sight. So, again, just be yourself. He knows your darkest secret, your deepest shame, your worst thought, your camouflaged motives, your stormy past and your vile imagination. Yet He loves you still and is calling you to be an X-Man. God chose Moses not because he committed murder and ran off to live in the wilderness for forty years, but because he humbled himself. Moses quit making excuses and walked in his calling.

God wants you to be faithful. I bet if I called your job, your boss would say you are a faithful employee. I mean you show up to work on time, sometimes you even work later than scheduled. You know your job and you do it well with little or no supervision. If I asked your co-workers or your spouse, they would all say you are faithful. If ever there was a time when you were not faithful as an X-Man you have died to it. When you come to God, He not only washes away your sin, but your tormenting guilt as well. Because you have accepted to die to your past, if asked, God would call you a faithful servant, not because you are impressive, but rather because you are submissive. Your Pastor would also call you faithful because you are an X-Man who died and was resurrected by Christ and not because you attend Church services every Sunday or you are one of the largest tithe payers.

I challenge you as men of God not to prejudge God the way you do people. Do not assume that open confrontation with God will be negative. Job had a confrontation with God and God had no problems answering Job? For you men who are saved and walking in your calling, learn a lesson from Job and do not get at ease with your life. You will never know when the devil will show up and ask the Lord to take His hedge from around you. It is when you become at ease that the devil will find a way to test your relationship and your walk as an X-Man. It is imperative regardless of what your friends come and tell you, that you keep the faith. Like Job, regardless of what your wife or your friends or other family members might suggest, keep the faith. You are an X-Man and if you hold strong onto your faith, God will bring you through and bless you.

I know I was lost in sin and I was trying everyday to impress the crowd. I was working in Church, singing in the choir and attending bible study every chance I got, but I was still living in my sins. If I had physically died while still living in Brookhaven, I probably would have had a big funeral attended by most of the public officials, present and former employees, my siblings, children, aunts, cousins, nephews and nieces and people from all races. They all would have come to pay their respects. The Minster probably would have talked about my church and community service and how much I adored my children, but nothing he would have said would have done my soul any heavenly good. Everything he would have said would have been based on the life I lived while I was busy trying to impress everyone, but God. He would not have mentioned the times I disappointed my pastor, embarrassed my family and brought humiliation to myself and my friends. He probably would not have mentioned my shortcomings. I am very glad that I didn't die before leaving Brookhaven, and that since that time, I have come to know Jesus personally. I am very glad I came to Beacon and God shined His searchlight on me and convicted my heart. I am so glad I did not die before that October 21st encounter with Jesus. Jesus looked beyond all that I had done and poured out His grace and mercy and granted me salvation. He looked at my broken spirit and said "We can rebuild him. We have the technology. We can make him stronger, faster, bolder; We can create in him a clean heart and renew his mind and spirit. He will be known as an X-Man." Are you not glad you are not dead yet? Are you not glad that if you don't have the right relationship with your savior, you can stop right now and take care of it?

It doesn't matter how far this natural life may take you, before it is all said and done, God said "every knee shall bow and every tongue shall confess that Jesus Christ is Lord." Former President Clinton had a 9-11 of his own. It was the day Clinton died and an X-Man was resurrected. Clinton stated on September 11, 1998: "I believe that to be forgiven more than sorrow is required-at least two more things. First a determination to change and to repair breaches of my own making. I have repented. Secondly, what my bible calls a "broken spirit" an understanding that I must have God's help to be the person that I want to be; a willingness to give the very forgiveness I seek; a renunciation of the pride and the anger which cloud judgment, I will continue on the path of repentance, seeking pastoral support and that of other caring people so that they can hold me accountable for my own commitment." X-Men at some point in your life, you will have to come face to face with yourself and choose whom you will serve. Once the choice is made you must let nothing cloud your judgment and know that your confession and conversion is the beginning and not the end of your transformation journey. After almost two terms in office, my favorite President was finally onto something.

You may be reading this book and feeling like a failure, but believe me, you are not. Maybe you feel misunderstood and downcast. Maybe you are unemployed and cannot get a job. Maybe evil has overwhelmed you and your to the point where you are asking God the timeless question "Why?" Maybe you have experienced a set back in your life. Trust me, God has a plan. The hardest thing in the world that I had to do was to face myself and call myself out and say "Edward you have been a liar, a thief, a deceiver, dishonest and adulterous person", and that's just the short list. The things I did to win cases or to push a deal through—only God can know. But despite my shortcomings God let me know that I was to become one of His disciples. I was to become an X-Man, a Soldier for Christ that my time for ministry had come. When I was trapped and possessed with evil spirits, God saved me. Every demon and unclean spirit in me He cast out.

St. Mark tells this very interesting story in the 5:2-8. He tells a story about a man who was living in the graveyard and always causing himself harm. Yea! Most of the harm in our lives is self inflicted. His lifestyle made an impression on everyone who knew him, but certainly not a good impression. Can you imagine a man running around half naked and cutting himself? The leading men in the community (you know the church goers and chamber of commerce members) had made numerous unsuccessful attempts to bind him with chains and tame him. However, when the man saw Jesus he immediately went and introduced himself. He cried out and begged that Jesus, the Son of the most high God, would stop his torment. Jesus looked at the man differently from the other men in the community. The men who tried to bind and tame him were concerned about his outer appearance for they saw him as an embarrassment, but Jesus looked at his heart. When Jesus spoke, the demons that had possessed the man immediately became subject to Him and He commmanded the unclean spirits to come out.

I was just like this man and so were some of you. I may not have been living in the graveyard, but I was certainly possessed by the devil. Yet when I met Jesus, He looked past my exterior and immediately diagnosed my trouble on the inside. X-Men when Jesus looks at you, He looks at your insides. He let me know that yes, He could use me, but He had to do an inside job on me first. After being confronted with the consequences of my sins and being exposed by God, my Father opened up His arms and said "welcome, my son who was lost has come home." I came home fired up and excited about telling my transformation message to anyone who would listen. I had gone full circle and it had taken me all of twelve years and twelve days to get there. X-Men when you come home, you still have not made an impression on God. You're coming home because God has finally made an impression on you. I thought initially, and several times since, that I couldn't make it, but then I remembered God had made no plans for my failure. "For I know the thoughts that I think toward you, says the Lord, thoughts of peace and not of evil, to give you a future and a hope" (*Jeremiah 29:11*). X-Men do not fear other men. X-Men do not worry about impressing the crowd. "The Lord is your helper; for what can man do to you?" (*Hebrew 13:6*).

X-Men it does not matter where you are coming from or where you are. God is waiting with open arms to welcome you to walk in the calling He has on your life. He could have taken your life, but He spared you one more day. *Romans 8:10* states "And if Christ be in you, the body is dead because of sin; but the spirit is life because of righteousness." God has not dealt with us according to our sins, nor rewarded us according to our iniquities. God has a plan for your life. He does not want you to lose your soul. Jesus asked the question, "What shall it profit a man to gain the whole world and lose his soul" (Matthew 16:26). Apostle Paul adds "For do I now persuade men, or God? Or do I seek to please men? For if I yet pleased men, I should not be the servant of Christ" (*Galatians 1:10*). Again, I ask, who are you trying to impress? Just die already! If anyone should attempt to bring your past back into your life for the sake of embarrassment, discouragement or to impress a crowd, it should be DOA-Dead On Arrival.

Again, I say, do not worry about the view of your self on earth; just concentrate on the view from above. Consider what God thinks of you when He looks down and sees your every deed. What kind of impression are you making?

SESSION SIX

When An X-man Falls In Love

"Love covers a multitude of Faults"

Love By Grace

Is your poor heart searching?
For that perfect love?
For that one true friend
You can always trust?

Do you need more joy?
Than the world can give?
Are you seeking peace?
And hope to live?
Then there's good news
For you, my friend;
There's such a love, and it never ends.

It's found in Jesus
God's precious Son,
His grace abounds
With peace and love.

Its yours for the asking,
Just ask in faith;
The love you long for Is yours by grace!
bY Jan McIntosh

What greater love is there than to be sentenced to death row and someone else agrees to die in your place (*See Romans 5:8*)**.** No greater love ever been expressed than the love Jesus Christ has shown for us all. Isn't it great to know that Christ made you and me beneficiaries to a Living Irrevocable Charitable Salvation Trust Fund over 2000 years ago. That's right, a Trust Fund was set up in your name on Calvary. Salvation is your birth right, but you must exercise the choice and chose. Barabbas is one of those biblical characters who usually do not make the Sunday Morning headlines as one of the good guys. But consider this, he was the first beneficiary of Calvary. Barabbas was a known terrorist, a rebel who had led a bloody murderous insurrection against Rome. When Jesus realized that the first person who was going to benefit from his death was a murderer, He could have spoken out and said no, hold up, wait a minute. He could have questioned whether or not Barabbas was worthy. Barabbas was still a sinner who had neither repented nor asked for forgiveness. However, despite the screaming crowd, our Savior never, ever said a mumbling word. X-Men, if Christ would allow Himself to be betrayed by one of His own disciples and then sacrifice His life for a terrorist, surely He made the choice to die for you and me. Now that's love.

Most of the time, when a man use the words "I Love You" it is in relation to getting a girl's attention and showing commitment. I heard one guy say the only time he ever said "I Love You" to a woman was at two o'clock in the morning—when nothing else would work. For some of you reading this book, the only time you have ever told God you loved Him was when you needed something and you thought you would lie, negotiate or barter with God to get it. You remember when you said, "Lord I'm sorry. Lord I surrender, Lord I promise, Lord I give up or Lord if You just help me this one last time." One can imagine God just smiling graciously and telling you, "yea right!" Remember that every time you come to God, He is looking at your heart. He knows every tomorrow. He is not someone you can bargain and barter with. However, if you say, Lord I love you, my God will test and prove you.

What does it mean to be an X-Man who has fallen in love with Christ? Love is often defined as a strong positive emotion of regard and affection; an intense attraction or attachment; in deep, tender, effable feeling. Love involves sacrifice and compromises where someone else's happiness is vital to your own. Love is often synonymous with affection, devotion, fondness or infatuation. Love means your doing everything you can to maintain a good relationship in an imperfect world. We hear numerous idioms with the word love, for example, all's fair in love and war, labor of love, misery loves company, no love lost, puppy love. My daughter's favorite movie is "Love and Basketball". However, my favorite idiom is, "Somebody up there loves me."

I envision that somebody up there to be Jesus whose love is unconditional. To truly love is to truly see God and to see God is to see love, for Jesus is love. X-Men, as you fall in Love with God, you will notice that your speech and actions will change and impact your future. No matter what, when you are in Love with God you can always go home. When you are in Love with God you can release some people from your life. When you are in Love with God you can lay aside the weight that has been holding you back from your calling. You can truly and sincerely separate yourself from your sinful past. When you are in Love with God you can tell others about the Living Water who gives unconditional love. When it comes to going after what you love in life, don't take no for an answer.

"Though, I speak with the tongues of men and of angels, and have not charity (love), I am become as sounding brass, or a tinkling cymbal. [2] And though I have the gift of prophecy, and understand all mysteries, and all knowledge; and though I have all faith, so that I could remove mountains, and have not charity; I am nothing. [3] And though I bestow all my goods to feed the poor, and though I give my body to be burned, and have not charity, it profited me nothing. [4] Charity suffered long, and is kind; charity envieth not; charity vaunted not itself, is not puffed up, [5] Doth not behave itself unseemly, seeketh not her own, is not easily provoked, thinketh no evil; [13] And now abideth faith, hope, charity, these three; but the greatest of these is charity" (*1 Corinthians 13:1-5 and 13*).

X-Men you should always love people and use things. Your daily walk should be an example of the character of love. As an X-Man you should love the unlovable as Christ loved you—*a charity case. Ephesians 2:8-10* states: "For by grace you have been saved through faith, and that not of yourselves; it is the gift of God. Not of works, lest anyone should boast. [F]or we are His workmanship, created in Christ Jesus for good works, which God prepared beforehand that we should walk in them."

How many times have you told someone, "I Love You?" In his song "When a Man Loves a Woman", Percy Sledge states: "When a man loves a woman, can't keep his mind on nothing else, He'd trade the world for the good thing he's found." It is ironic and unfortunate that a man would give up the world for a woman, but will not give up or separate himself from the world for God. How many times have you told God, "I Love You?" Peter was asked three times by Jesus, "Do you love me?" Abraham was tested to see if he loved his son Isaac more than he loved God. Your children cannot be your god. Your wife cannot be your god. Only God can be your God. When you are an X-Man God has to be first in your life. Your character has to be consistent with the character of God. This process is not going to be easy, thus X-Men must pool their strength and resources together always encouraging one another and working diligently to live for Christ. X-Men are representatives of Jesus to a world of men who have not yet been transformed. X-Men today is your day ordained by God to exercise your salvation, tear down strongholds and lay aside every weight that so easily besets you. Do not let Satan rob you of your joy by bringing up your past loves, such as women, drugs, money and fame—tell the devil you've got a new love. Don't let him bring old stuff into your life and cause stressful situations that will lure you into old habits.

X-Men you are in a race for your lives with no time outs left and no time to lose. Because of your new love for Christ and your constant battle with Satan you will always be challenged, convicted, encouraged and inspired. Do not make excuses, straddle the fence or become lacking in your commitment. Your decline is not inevitable, through Christ you are now a committed and thriving X-Man. You have hell to shun and heaven to gain. As X-Men you are required to fall and stay in love with God and face destiny. In order to stay in love we must learn to guard our hearts and thoughts for Christ. Paul wrote; "For though we walk in the flesh, we do not war after the flesh. For the weapons of our warfare are not carnal, but mighty through God to the pulling down of strong holds; Casting down imaginations, and every high thing that exalteth itself against the knowledge of God, and bringing into captivity every thought to the obedience of Christ" (*2 Corinthians 10:3-5*). Do not let the devil cause you to lose your love for God, remain in love with and obedient to God, and stay in church.

There is an old saying that, "Women go to Church. Men go to football games", because men are competitive. This competitive nature, despite the new love of God love a man feels for his wife, has created new church dilemmas. Men are now faced with problems with the same women they love at home, because these women are operating in the church on a different level than the men are. You would think we are busy enough dealing with our own relationship problems instead of fighting for position in the church. But this is what happens when we lose focus of the love of our lives. We entertain problems that are negligible. I have seen love turn into resentment allegedly all in the name of Christ and the Church. I have noticed that the biggest problem for most men who are not secure in themselves is that they believe women have taken over the church. Statistically, women often make up about 80 percent of regular church attendees. There are even churches that are struggling with whether women should be Evangelist, Ministers, Pastors, etc. There is no doubt that men and women are different emotionally, but not necessarily different spiritually.

So what is the role of men and women in the church? Is it to gain position, power or a chance to display their natural talent or ability? The answer is NO! The church is a place for people to congregate to learn and worship and to become true followers of Christ, man or woman. Your soul does not compete with women nor should it be offended by their overwhelming presence. Don't confuse the means with the end. Why even fight over the role of women when we are all in this fight together? **Galatians 3:28** states "There is neither Jew nor Greek, there is neither bond nor free, there is neither male nor female: for ye are all one in Christ Jesus." This verse points out the fact that the spiritual standing of every human being regardless of nationality, class or gender is the same. We are all called to become X-Men. The playing field is truly leveled at the cross with equal access to all.

If we take a closer look, even when we get our roles straight, the real problem is competitiveness, in that men do not like to be outdone. While women are busy learning relationship building and management, men were busy learning how to play games. Men play games because they are used to events having a winner and a loser. However, worship is not a competitive sport. Nevertheless, X-Women, even without position or status have been out running X-Men in the name of Jesus for a long time. The reason for this is that X-Women have got this love thing down pack. Love with Christ requires some relationship building. Most of the time in the bible when women needed something from Christ, because of their love for Him they pressed to get to Him. When the men want or need something from Christ, because of their emotional resistance to admit the need for help, men wait for Christ to come to them. It was the women who went early Sunday morning to visit the tomb of Jesus. It was the woman who washed Jesus feet. It was the women who first saw Jesus after His resurrection. X-men it is time for you to overcome your problem with women in the church and take your rightful place as Head of the family and leaders in your local congregation. That's right X-Men God created you as the Head, so quite acting like you are the feet! Look at it like this, if Adam had been a leader, we would not be in this mess. It is time for you to be a leader, and leaders lead. It is time for you to act like Peter when he found out that Jesus has risen. You need to take off running like you never ran before. You need to change from a being a football player to a track star. Instead of suiting up for battle you need to dress down so you can run for your life. I imagine switchblade-toting Peter dropped the sword he had in the garden so he could run. I imagine he stopped cursing so he could run. I imagine he stopped denying Christ so he could run. I know David dressed down and took off the armor so he could easily run toward Goliath. David did not limit himself and he did not limit God. X-Men, it is time for you to take off running and come crashing through the brick wall, fly into action and lead the charge for Christ.

Jesus and his disciples came to the city of Samaria, Jesus sat down outside the city next to Jacob's Well. After the disciples were gone into the city to buy some food and supplies a woman came to the Well to draw water. Jesus, being thirsty, asked the woman to give him a drink. The woman replied, "don't you know that Jews have nothing to do with Samaritans?" (Kind of like some so-called elitist proud saints who would have nothing to do with sinners, rather than be loveable saints). Jesus answered her, "If you knew the gift of God, and who it is that you were talking to you would ask Me for water." Jesus told her that whosoever drank of the Well's water would thirst again, but if she drank of the water He was giving her, a Well would spring up inside of her into everlasting life. When she asked Him for His water, Jesus began to tell her all about her past. He brought all of her sins before her and she was forced to face herself in the mirror and make a decision. After being confronted and provoked regarding her salvation, the woman chose Jesus. The scripture teaches us that God is a spirit and they that worship God must worship him in spirit and in truth (*See John 4: 4-26*).

Men, if it is competition that drives you, here's the part that should make every X-Man who knows and confesses Jesus Christ as His Lord and Savior to strive for the rest of his life to bring new recruits to Christ. *John 4:27* states, "And upon this came His disciples, and marveled that He talked with the woman: yet no man said, What seekest thou? Or, Why talkest Thou with her?" X-Men, do you see the problem here? These men knew Christ and even claimed to love Him; they had walked with Him, talked with Him, and watched Him perform miracles. They went into the city knowing fully well Whom they had left at the Well and they didn't tell anyone.

They didn't say, to the people they had met in the city, "hey, you know the man with unconditional love who healed the sick, gave sight to the blind, fed the 5000, walked on the water and calmed the sea, the one who made the lame walk, the deaf hear, cleansed the lepers and raised the dead, the One who can forgive you and wash all your sins away—He is sitting right out side the City at the Well of Jacob." They neither said a word nor brought back anyone with them. They just went to McDonalds got their Happy meals and walked back out of town.

In *verse 28 and 29 John* wrote: "The woman then left her water pot, and went her way into the city, and saith to the men, Come, see a man, which told me all things that ever I did: is not this the Christ?" The bible states "let the redeemed of the Lord say so." (*Psalm 107:2*). If you love and confess Jesus as your Lord and Savior then you should be telling somebody about Him. X-Men it is inconceivable that you would know Christ is sitting outside the city and not tell it everywhere you go. It is incomprehensible that your Pastor is sharing the living word every Sunday and you don't invite strangers to service. X-Men do not let the woman at the Well out run you for Christ. Get a drink of the living water and let everybody you meet know where you got it. For the love of God, run the race. You can be anything, do anything, change anything, you just have to drink of the water. You are an X-Man and you can do all things through Christ Jesus. Your efforts can change lives. Your ingenuity and your passion should motivate others to follow in your footsteps. But you have to learn how to love and lead. Leaders lead by example.

You X-Men who profess to know and love Jesus, how enthusiastic have you been to spread the good news of our risen Lord and Savior whom you claim to love? How many of you after hearing a great word from the Lord, left Church and went and talked to your friends and said come see a man. I realize that getting your life back on track, after a dramatic change in direction is not an easy thing. You should have seen me when Christ exposed all of my sins in less than two weeks. I realize that there is guilt, shame and humiliation when you reflect on other relationships. Maybe you have hurt someone and you are not sure you'll be able to look the person you've wronged in the eye. Or you think you cannot go back and confront those friends you used to hang out with before you were saved. However, once you do, you'll see: what happened was not a mistake, not an accident, not a fantasy or a dream, but—"come see a man, come get a drink of the Living Water".

When you fall in Love with Christ like the woman who left her water pot, there are some things you will need to leave behind. When you fall in Love you'll be telling friends and strangers to come see a man. It will be just like fire burning in your bones. (*See Jeremiah 20:9*). If you want Jesus to confess you on Judgment day then I advise you to get busy confessing Him. Jesus stated: "Whosoever therefore shall confess Me before men, him will I confess also before My father which is in heaven" (*Matthew 10:32*).

When you fall in love, you will be a help to your brothers. In *Luke*, Christ tells the story of the Good Samaritan who took care of the man who had been beaten and robbed without consideration of his race or status; he was just someone who needed help. As the Bible tells us, he was not the only man who walked by and saw the injured man or noticed his predicament. Of all the men who walked by, only the Samaritan showed love. How many times have you walked by a person in need of help? How many times have you had the opportunity to witness to your fellow brother, but instead you just walked past. How many times have you looked at the way a person lives and been judgmental about his or her condition? What you ought to say is: "There I go, but for the grace of God." How many opportunities have you been given to be of service to your community or Church and you refused? How many times have you asked God for something and your request was denied?

Society teaches us that the major obligation of man is to earn money and support his dependent loved ones. The state even mandates it as a legal obligation. Timothy wrote that a man who does not take care of his family is less than an infidel and has denied the faith (See 1 Timothy 5:8). However, I submit that the major obligation of X-Men is to Love God and love others as Christ loved them. In America, men are culturally groomed to blame themselves for what they believe to be their failures as men. On this point, I can agree with the world. If we, men, do not take credit for our failures we cannot take credit for past or future successes. As leaders you can delegate almost everything accept responsibility. You cannot begin to be anchored in Christ without taking responsibility for your actions. In times like these, X-Men need a savior and an anchor—Jesus. This is not the time to suppress your fears and allow confusion or anger to be determinative of your being your own master. It is time to stop and turn to Jesus. It doesn't matter what your struggle is, He is faithful and just to forgive. It does not matter how many times your integrity has been compromised. It does not matter the number of your past sins. His divinity can never and will never be compromised. Christ will always consider you His child, because He knows you are worthy of His unconditional love.

SESSION SEVEN

Be Afraid-Be Very Afraid!

"If you are scared, just say you're scared."

I understand that we often forget that God loves us and He will protect and keep us from all harm. I realize that so many men are afraid and just afraid too admit it. Back in my neighborhood, we'd say, "If you are scared just say you're scared." In 2001 the Gallup Organization asked Americans what they were most afraid of. The number one answer from 51 per cent of the people polled, was snakes. You'd think Adam and Eve should have read the poll back in Eden. Sure could have saved us all a lot of trouble. God, who is love (*1 John 4:8*), expresses His love by giving us the freedom to choose; but the wrong choice will always have adverse consequences.

All of us experience fear in our lives. Bottom line, fear happens. I remember being really scared in the fifth grade. I was afraid of a bully who wanted to beat me up after school, because I wouldn't give him my basketball. It seemed like everybody in school knew I was suppose to get into a fight that afternoon. Compared to me, at the time, the bully was a giant and at least three years older than I was. He was in special education and spent his days terrorizing the entire fourth and fifth grade. I was shaking with fear and my stomach was in knots, dreading when the bell would ring and school would be dismissed. When the bell finally rang, I took off running: I ran all the way home while the bully chased after me. I lived approximately two miles from the school and I tell you, I was running as fast as my little feet would carry me.

Unfortunately for me, my father was at home waiting in the front yard with some of his friends. He saw me running and before I could get in the house he grabbed me by my collar and said, "where are you going so fast?" I was out of breath and all I could do was point up the street toward the bully. My father stated, "put your books down and go back up the street and see what he wants!" I already knew what the bully wanted, so going back up the street in my opinion really was unnecessary. You would think the bully would shut up and go away seeing that my family was in the front yard. However, this guy would not let up. He was talking and cursing at me. He was calling my father and my mother names. Back in the day, when a person said, "Yo mama!" it was time to fight, but given the circumstances I was willing to make an exception. But my father was watching, and he had made it clear I could not come back home until I had gone back up the street. I was little David and the bully was my Goliath. I picked up a small brick from the yard and hit the bully with it. Before he could recover, I was all over him with my fists like white on rice. The neighbors had to pull us apart. My father was just standing in the yard smiling with his friends saying, "that's my boy!, that's my boy!" Men, I know you get scared sometimes, but every time you run, know that you father God is watching. He is watching and he's demanding that you go and face your fears. Remember it is not the size of the dog in the fight, but the size of the fight in the dog.

We, Men sometimes get so scared that we sometimes start running scared. We should be calling God for help, but instead we call 911. We chose to exclude God from areas of our lives, because we are afraid He cannot handle it. **The same thing happens when we exclude things from our spouse or people close to us, thinking that they cannot handle the truth.** We think like Jack Nicolson in the movie "A Few Good Men" we tell God, "You want the truth, you can't handle the truth!" Excluding God from any area of our lives is risky, since we are left in bondage of sin in one form or another. Nothing we do, even in private is hidden from God. Don't you want God to look down from heaven and say, "this is My son or daughter in whom I am well pleased?" So why are we afraid? Afraid that the future is set in stone. Afraid to ask for help, because to admit need is to give into weakness. Afraid that you've done something so terrible or so wrong that you cannot be forgiven. The psalmist wrote, "Thou has set our iniquities before thee, our secret sins in the light of Thy countenance" (*Psalm 90:8*). X-Men do not be afraid of being laughed at or become paranoid about what someone else might think. Do not faint in the day of adversity, be strong. Remember your father is watching, so make Him proud.

Do not be afraid my brothers, for God has not given you the spirit of fear. If you fear God you will not need to fear anyone else. Fear constricts life so much that scientist have given our irrational fear a special name called phobias. Phobias like agraphobia the fear of sexual abuse; agateophobia the fear of insanity; an Aglophobia the fear of pain; and atychiphobia the fear of failure, just to name a few. Fear has become so prevalent in our society that one of the most popular reality shows is entitled "Fear Factor". If you are an X-Man; fear is not a factor for you. No longer should you be afraid of rejection. If you sincerely repent and pray to God, he will never reject you. The old saying that the only thing to fear is fear itself is a lie. God has brought you into a new reality called "Survivor". You are a survivor of sin and shame, worry and anxiety. You are a survivor of the graveyard of your life. You are a survivor of the cancers that have been eating away at your soul. You are a survivor of abandonment, anger, contentment, depression, disappointment, uncertainty, outrage, pride and vengeance. X-Man, you are a Survivor, and fear is not a factor!

Luke 12:5 teaches us who we should fear. "But I will show you whom you should fear: Fear Him who, after He has killed, has power to cast into hell; yes, I say to you, fear Him!" X-Men take heed and be aware of covetousness, for one's life does not consist in the abundance of the things he possesses. Fear of God is where the pathway of your evolution begins (*see Proverbs 1:7*). Your transformation is measured only by what you do for Christ. Don't let the devil allow you to be fearful. Fear cripples the heart and mind and traps your soul. X-Men do not fear or worry, because you have been found worthy. Do not worry about your life. "And which of you (X-Men) by worrying can add one cubit to his statute?" (*Luke 12:25*). Remember God has got your back. Whatever it is you can't handle, surrender it to God and move forward in faith.

Do not let anyone convince you to be afraid of coming to Christ. Don't listen to the negative internal voice that tells you, "you can't". For faith is the substance of things hoped for. Hope is a powerful tool especially when you are afraid. Hope never quits. Hope forces us in spite of our fear to never give up. Hope in Christ will empower and strengthen your heart. The woman with the issue of blood for 12 years had hope. "The eyes of the Lord are in every place, beholding the evil and the good (*Proverbs 15:3*). So there you have it, God already knows your every deed. Your fear of men need not be pathological. "For God hath not given us the spirit of fear; but of power, and of love, and of a sound mind" (*2 Timothy 1:7*). X-Men are worthy of salvation. "The fear of man bringeth a snare: but whoso putteth his trust in the Lord shall be safe" (*Proverbs 29:25*). You are a new creature, your past sins are forgiven. You have been granted immunity. Jesus doesn't look at your past He looks at your present faith and your hope. "Wherefore neither thought I myself worthy to come unto thee: but say in a word, and my servant shall be healed. For I also am a man set under authority, having under me soldiers, and I say unto one, Go and he goeth; and to another, Come, and he cometh; and to my servant, Do this, and he doeth it. When Jesus heard these things, he marveled at him, and turned him about, and said unto the people that followed him, I say unto you, I have not found so great faith, no, not in Israel (*Luke 7:7-9*). X-Men don't worry, there is nothing you need that God cannot give. There is nothing your dealing with that God want bring you through. If you are experiencing some fear or failure don't run away—run toward God.

X-Men, now knowing you the way only you and God do, how will you finish the race of life if you died right now? Will you be saved or condemned? What is the sum of all your fears? *Luke 13:23-24:* Then one said to Him, "Lord, are there few who are saved?" And He said to them, "Strive to enter through the narrow gate, for many, I say to you, will seek to enter and will not be able." Men and Women, if you die tonight and unsaved, be afraid. Don't worry about what people will say about you. You need to be concerned about what God will say. If you are not striving to make God a part of your daily life, be afraid. If you die without a Godly legacy, be afraid. If you keep giving God excuses and fail to make in on Judgment day, be afraid. If you are a sinner and tomorrow never comes, be afraid. X-Men now is the time to confront your fears and face your future calling with strength and courage. You are in the process of your transformation: fear should not be a factor.

SESSION EIGHT

Process Of Becoming Qualified?
Who Is In Control: Pride, Repentance, Humility?

I remember not too long ago when one of my friends who was looking into a new career contacted me for some advice. He was concerned that the position he most desired would not want him because of his lack of qualifications in some skills and his over-qualification in others. In his mind he was only qualified to do one thing. He was wondering if he was in the minority by wanting peace and happiness in his career. As a recruiter and counselor, I quickly informed him that approximately ten percent of adults in the workforce change occupations each year and about 4 million members of the work force change employers per month. In his previous career, opportunities appeared serendipitously or seemed to develop through contacts and networking. But now, he was drafting resumes, visiting employment services and career counselors, reading the wanted ads and conducting electronic job searches. He was attempting to acquire new career skills, new contacts, new attitudes and behavior. He wasn't sure he knew what recruiters were looking for. He hadn't considered that recruiters are looking for liabilities—not assets. They are looking for reasons to exclude you. X-Men, if you are looking for a job you might as well find one that you love. After all if you're going to spend 50-75 percent of your time working, why not do something you love? Why not do something that makes you happy and excited? Why not live with a purpose and find a position where you are able to genuinely impact the people around you? Find your dream job, come work for God.

Christ has a different outlook on what it takes to qualify someone for service versus what society thinks. Society's view of success always seems to carry certain prerequisites for qualification, such as age, education or years of experience. The very notion of becoming qualified assumes an element of deficiency, a lack of skill, training, talent, or intellect that ordinarily renders one fit for accomplishment. Let's face it, if you want the job, you've got to prove you are qualified. A Lawyer has to graduate law school and pass the Bar to be qualified to practice. A Doctor, Accountant, Engineer, Teacher, Psycologist or Pharmacist would have to hold certain certifications before working in the chosen profession. Even in grammar school, one must master certain basic skills before advancing to the next grade. Some believe that one must have a degree in Theology from an accredited Seminary, before one can preach or serve in ministry. As a result, we sometimes convince ourselves that we cannot be successful in certain areas because we lack the societal prerequisites. However, Christ concluded that God qualifies and justifies those whom He has called for service.

Looking back at some of our biblical heroes, we can see that it was not by chance that Moses survived Pharaoh's order to have all newborn sons killed. Nor was it at Moses' command that his rod turned into a serpent, the river became blood, locust took over Egypt, the red sea parted into two or that manna fell from heaven. It was at the command of God that he became qualified for service. It was not David's own strength that defeated Goliath. It was not Elisha that miraculously transformed the poisoned water supply into a clean spring in Jericho. It wasn't because of him that a curse fell on his attackers in Bethel, that the poor widow's supply of oil increased or that the iron head floated in the water of the Jordan River. It was because of that "double portion of Elijah's Spirit", the Holy Spirit of God whom he inherited at Elijah's chariot home going *(See 2 Kings chapters 3, 4 and 6)*. When you do something great or spectacular in ministry, remember you didn't do it; it was God who qualified you.

At this point you may be saying o.k., I am ready, but I don't know where to start. I have the faith; I have shaven off my fear, but now what? I don't believe I'm qualified to talk and lead someone to Christ. I cannot quote Bible verses or I am not well versed in scripture. I don't know if I am capable of speak about deliverance. I don't know if I have what it takes to accomplish the task before me. I know when I start speaking, they are going to bring up my past. God says to you, don't worry about your qualifications or credentials. When God calls you, He will equip you just like He did Moses. Just like He has done since the beginning of time. When God introduced himself to Moses, He said, "I AM." God told Moses, go tell Pharaoh I AM sent you. X-Men, that is what God is saying to you, whatever you need, He says "I AM." I am a present help in times of trouble. I am the one who called you out of darkness into the marvelous light. I am the one who saved and justified you. I am Alpha and Omega. I am your healer and your provider. God is everything, so stand justified and forgiven through grace. Don't let Satan keep you handcuffed to your past.

Like my sister Laura taught me, "don't get stressed, use your I AM." I = Ignore the small things. A = Accept the things that can't be changed. M = Move on and let God handle it. "All things work together for good to them that love God, to them who are called according to his purpose. For whom he did foreknow, he also did predestinate to be conformed to the image of his son, that he might be the first born among many brethren. Moreover whom he did predestinate, them he also justified: and whom he justified, them he also glorified. What shall we then say to these things? X-Men if God be for us, who can be against us? He that spared not his own Son, but delivered him up for us all, how shall he not with him also freely give us all things? Who shall lay any thing to the charge of God's elect? It is God that Justifieth?" *(Romans 8:28-33)*.

X-Men, God will equip you with His Amazing Grace for the Amazing Race that He has set before you; all you have to do is ask. God tells us in *James 1:5* "[I]f any (X-Man) lack wisdom, let him ask of God, that giveth to all men liberally, and unbraided not; and it shall be given him." Remember you are an X-Man chosen by God. We are further instructed in *John 15:16* that we did not choose Him, but rather Christ chose us and that whatsoever you shall ask of the Father in His name, He shall give it you. X-Men God would not choose you and then refuse to equip and qualify you. In fact He chose you before the foundation of the world, at a time when you couldn't choose Him.

As you know by now, everything is a process. The first step in the process of being qualified is exchanging your prideful spirit for a humble spirit. God is waiting for you to celebrate the funeral of your pride. The second step is to repent and pray. Remember the bible says that an X-Man should always pray. The third step is to train for your calling. After all, you cannot lead someone to Christ, if you don't know the requirements yourself. The final step is becoming Meek and Humble. Pride is believing that we have achieved what in reality God and others have achieved for us. Prayer is the act of communicating with God. Repentance is an act of salvation based on faith. Repentance requires a change in mind, attitude, lifestyle and it results in forgiveness. Humility and Meekness is recognizing that God and others are actually responsible for the achievements in your life. Humility causes one not to seek public acclaim. As the Chinese would say, "don't worry about holding a high position, worry rather about playing your proper role." X-Men, God wants you to die to your pride that you might live a humble life through Him. God recognizes that one of the hardest things for a man to do is give up control of or to lay down his pride. Our problem, X-Men, is that we are pretty self-centered. We think the world revolves around us. News flash—it doesn't. Most of us at some point tend to walk around as if we have an **S** on our chest. Notice I said X-Man, not Superman. **S**uperman you are not, but a **S**ervant you can become. *Philippians 4:13* does not state that you can do all things, because you are the man, it says you can do all things because you know the Man. Christ is that man. Humble yourself and let Christ take the reigns. Do not pat yourself on the back, but give honor to Him from whom all blessings flow.

As we examine the issue of pride, we must ask ourselves some tough questions. How do you teach a proud man anything at all? How do you counsel a man who thinks he is Superman? Where did he learn his egotistical pride? What school did he go to? Who was his teacher? Who infected God's creation with such a fatal disease? The survey says,—***drum roll please***—Satan. It started when God decided to create a whole new species called man. But before Adam, God had created Angels and one of those Angels was named Lucifer. When Lucifer found out about the creation of Adam, to be made "a little lower than the angels" *(Hebrew 2:7)*, he rebelled. Here is a super-being, *(not Superman but an Archangel,)* not limited by the laws of gravity or other mundane restraints, whose rebellion was motivated out of the pride of his own heart. "Thou wast perfect in thy ways from the day that thou wast created, till iniquity was found in thee" . . . "Thine heart was lifted up because of thy beauty, thou hast corrupted thy wisdom by reason of thy brightness . . ."*(Ezekiel 28:15, 17)*. Since that great fall, Satan has infected man with the same self-serving pride. As X-Men we are told: "Be sober, be vigilant; because your adversary the devil, as a roaring lion, walketh about, seeking whom he may devour" *(1 Peter 5:8)*. Pride has infected the whole creation, and no one is exempt. Pride is what twisted your cross to an *X* to start with. This is why our Lord Jesus had to come and die on the cross and save the day. It all began with Lucifer and his pride.

For most, this infection has become too deep to reach through psychological counseling. There are just some things that a session with Dr. Phil cannot cure. It is outside the reach of human effort one that no medication prescribed will provide a cure. It defies all intellectual restraints. It is a frightful disease of the heart. A proud man is infected all his ways. To combat pride an X-Man must "look not every man on his own thing, but every man also on the things of others" *(Phil. 2:4)*. X-Men must not love the world, neither the things that are in the world. "If any man loves the world, the love of the father is not in him. For all that is in the world, the lust of the flesh, the lust of the eyes, and the pride of life, is not of the father, but is of the world" *(1 John 2:15-16)*. I can hear someone saying now, "oh, but that's not me, pride is not my problem. If you said it then I submit that pride itself has blinded your eyes and caused you to believe that you are not subject to its infection. You remember that it was through pride that Adam and Eve rebelled in the garden of Eden *(Rev. 12:9)*. Pride goeth before destruction and a haughty spirit before a fall. Better it is to be of a humble spirit, then to divide the spoils with the proud" *(Proverbs 16:18)*. Pride is a resident evil and every time you kill it, if you are not careful, it will rise up again stronger than it ever was before. Pride makes a man believe he is self-sufficient thus unteachable. Pride has a way of keeping you from growing and blinding you from seeing your shortcomings. In order for an X-Man to continue in his transformation, he must confess the sin of pride, kill it and bury it deep.

I know even now someone is still boasting, "But that's not me. I pray and read His word every day, do many good works and I'm active in the Church." If this is you, then you have a prideful spirit that you need to confess and die to. You think you are a member of Who's Who in Church, serving as God's self-appointed Kingdom Cop and a recent inductee into the "Bible Study know it All" Hall of Fame. Yea, you know who you are! You have been in the church showing off your talents, singing, dancing or preaching for your glory, verses for the glory of God. In short, if you are not willing to admit your pride, then I submit that your pride has gotten in the way. Do you think you are exempt, that you have long ago been removed from a prideful heart, since you trusted Jesus as your savior? Do you honestly believe, that one trip to the altar would do? Are you so caught up in your pride that you cannot pray and repent? Is it impossible for you to stand up and say, "Yes, I am a proud man." Lord have mercy on my proud soul. I have rebelled against you in my deepest being. I have done my own thing, even in the Church. I have been deceived by the devil, even after coming to the altar, even after trusting Jesus for salvation. I have been lifted up in pride. Please give me meekness and humility." X-Men, if it is deliverance from pride that you seek, God will give you the desires of your heart, but you must first ask.

James 4:6 says, "God resisteth the proud . . ." X-Men, if God is for you, it does not make any difference who is against you; but if God is resisting you it does not make any difference who is for you. If you are proud, God will resist you. James the brother of Jesus tells us that God "giveth grace unto the humble." What is grace? Simply put, grace is the desire and the power that God gives us to live in harmony with His principles. The way to deal with pride and to get more grace is to humble ourselves by submitting to God's authority for our lives. *James 4:7 continues*, "Submit yourselves therefore to God. Resist the devil and he will flee from you." X-Men if you are going to wage an effective spiritual warfare then you must submit every area of your life to God's control. For every area that God does not control, Satan and his demons will. If you are looking to be qualified by God, it is time for you to chose who you want to be in control. In the midst of battle, who are you prepared to follow?

Warfare causes one to commit and become qualified for service. Men who have served or are serving in the military certainly understand the transformation qualifying process of X-Men as Soldiers for Christ. The Men's Ministry at Springfield Baptist is called Soldiers for Christ. The reason behind the name is that the aim of any good soldier is to satisfy the one who enlisted him. Jesus stated in Luke 6:40 ". . . everyone who is perfectly trained will be like his teacher." I am glad Jesus died for me. I am excited that He recruited me. I am proud to wear the uniform of Servant-Christ-Man, for my **X** is now a mark of distinction. Most soldiers join the armed services looking for a career, looking for structure, discipline, focus and purpose. Regardless of the branch of service, the powers that be will take you as they find you and transform you into the soldier you need to be. Whether it is with the military or with Jesus, all you have to do to join is answer the call of the recruiter. The first thing for any enlisted recruit is basic training-the time to be broken, humbled and retrained.

Every branch of the service has its slogan to attract new recruits and informs the enlisted that there is a qualifying process. The Air Force wants you to "Aim High." The Marines are looking, "For a Few Good Men"-the Few, the Proud, the Marines. The Navy wants you to "Be all you Can Be", where the career is not just a Job but an Adventure. You can join the Army and become an "Army of One" or if you are just dying to be "Part of the Action", join the Coast Guard. However, in a world of difficulty and hardness no slogan is more compelling than that expressed by Paul to be a good Soldier of Christ Jesus by fulfilling the great commission of sharing the truth of Christianity. If you are in Law Enforcement and you have sworn to "Protect and Serve" I encourage you to serve Jesus by teaching others by the quality of your Christian life. I entreat you as a Soldier for Christ not to go M.I.A. (Missing in Action) in the midst of the WAR. Do not receive a dishonorable discharge on Judgment Day due to lack of commitment in service or your inability to complete the basis training.

The final step in the qualification process of a soldier is Humility. Humility requires one to die to self-will, arrogance and self-assertiveness. Jesus said, "I am meek and lowly in heart" *(Matthew 11:29,30)*. Having come to earth as a man, Jesus humbled Himself and became obedient, even to the point of dying on the cross *(Philippians 2:8)*. Humility is important because the Holy Spirit cannot be cultivated without it. Humility requires meekness. Meekness does not imply weakness rather strength under control. How could one be patient and submissive in the trials and difficulties of life if not meek? How could one be kind toward opponents if he were not humble and meek? How could one be patient toward all, especially the body of Christ, if not humble and meek? How could one feel brotherly kindness except through meekness? How could one be Godlike except he possessed humility? How could one be loving in the spiritual sense without meekness and humility? X-Men as you continue on your transformation journey, meekness and humility must abound in your heart, so that the other fruits of the Spirit can be cultivated. Humility toward God is an admission that we need help from someone far greater than we are. Remember the devil will always be perched on your shoulder, whispering in your ear and encouraging you to be self-centered, egotistical and proud. So humble yourself and be submissive toward God.

Despite actions by Satan, your humility and determination is what God will use to qualify you for a successful ministry. *Luke 14:11* teaches us "For whoever exalts himself will be humbled, and he who humbles himself will be exalted." Have you ever had a humbling experience? Humility requires you to get rid of your ego and bury your pride. Humility will always come before honor. Some are born humble-minded and others self-conceited. Sometimes humility will come swiftly like with Apostle Paul on the road to Damascus or it could be like Moses' and take up to 40 years. For others like my father, it may even take longer. My father did not become humble until he was 67 years old and on his death bed. He was dying of lung cancer in Kings Daughter's Hospital in Brookhaven in 1992 when he finally laid it all on the altar and accepted Christ in his life. He had lived sixty-seven years in sin. I mean there were times he could raise hell in an empty room—so to speak. Even today, if the Gallup Organization polled citizens in Brookhaven for the most feared and prideful men to ever walk its streets, my father's name would certainly be at the top of the list.

My father was a proud man. His life story reminds me of the life of King Manasseh as recorded in *2 Kings 21:1 and 2 Chronicles 33*. Manasseh, one would say, was hell on wheels. He was on his way to hell in a hand basket during his fifty-five-year reign. The scriptures state that he did evil in the sight of the Lord. He did more evil than all of the Amorites before him. As you may recall, Manasseh is the one who killed the prophet Isaiah because he didn't want to hear the word of God. But after fifty-five years, God brought judgment against him, put him in prison and took his Kingdom. It was then and only then that Manasseh finally humbled himself. He buried his pride, his past and turned his face toward God and sincerely prayed and pleaded for forgiveness. After fifty-five years, God restored him back to his kingdom. Can you believe it, after fifty-five years of raising hell, worshipping idols, practicing witchcraft, and murdering, Manasseh died an X-Man. My father lived just like any man, a sinner. He had shot, stabbed, gambled, lied, stolen, indulged in alcohol and drugs, abused my mother occasionally, committed adultery, and committed other nameless and faceless sins, but he died an X-Man. Can you believe it? Manasseh and my father, R.W. Benson, Sr. were the same age when they experienced an epiphany in Christ, 67. Both Manasseh and my father, given their extensive years of living in their sins, could have been the poster men for X-Men. Now then, how long will it take before you become humble? Remember that if you do not humble yourself, God can and will humble you.

In the book of **Hosea** we see a truly humbling, loving and qualifying experience. Although Hosea was already working for God, he did not possess the level of humility sufficient for him to understand why God kept forgiving Israel. We find that the people of Israel had been unfaithful and had turned away from God and were worshipping Baal. Hosea began to think he should be the one to decide how many times God should forgive. God took an opportunity to further qualify Hosea and demonstrate the incredible, unconditional love that he had for the people of Israel, by sending Hosea through a Continuing Christian Education course (CCE). The story is told how Hosea was instructed to go down to the Red light district and marry a prostitute named Gomer. Talking about "breakin" a brother down. Can you imagine how Hosea must have felt? Nevertheless, against his personal desire, understanding, wisdom, judgment and convictions, and knowing that his boys were going to talk and ridicule him, Hosea put aside his pride and did what God had commanded. After Hosea married and had children with Gomer, Gomer decided to go back to her old way of living as a prostitute. But every time she left, Hosea went and found her and brought her back home and forgave her infidelity. Every time Hosea looked at Gomer he was reminded of God's love for Israel. He was reminded of how he had once looked down on Gomer. He was reminded of God's forgiveness. Hosea's marriage became a symbol of the unconditional love and forgiveness that God has for the people of God and the CCE he will put us through to keep us qualified for service. It was not until Hosea had lived through such an experience that God could truly continue to use him.

2 Chronicles 7:14 states, "If my people, (X-Men) which are called by my name, shall humble themselves, and pray, and seek my face, and turn from their wicked ways; then will I hear from heaven, and will forgive their sin, and will heal their land." Its amazing what God will do to humble and qualify you. I remember that 21st day of October, being stopped dead in my tracks by a police officer for missing an inspection sticker on my car. I humbly gave the officer my license only to find out that there was a warrant out for my arrest. Despite having friends and relatives in the Police and Sheriff Department it was a warrant I knew absolutely nothing about. The officer handcuffed me and placed me in the back of his patrol car. I was taken to the station and was told that because it was Friday afternoon, they could not get much information other than it was an active warrant and they had to hold me until I could see the Judge. I was taken to jail where I spent nine days in general population before being transported to another facility, where I spent an additional three days. I was spending time in jail for something I had not done. Yet I was remembering all the things that I had done wrong that could have landed me in prison years ago. Nevertheless, there I was, chained both hand and feet as I was transported by bus from place to place. I slept on the floor or on the seat. I could not shave or take a bath. Because of the chains, I had to be creative to use the bathroom. I had heard of the guarantee of protection from cruel and unusual punishment under the Eighth Amendment, but I was unprepared for that experience. However, in retrospect, I believe Manasseh as well as so many others who have served longer sentences than I, had it worse.

When I was initially arrested my primary concern was how **I** could fix my dilemma. How **I** knew the right things to say or the right people to call. I said, **if I** could just talk to the Chief of Police or someone at the Sheriff's department. **If I** could see the District Attorney. **If I** could just get to Brookhaven. **If I.** I realized **I** sounded like Satan when he said in his heart, "**I** will ascend into heaven, **I** will exalt my throne above the stars of God: **I** will sit upon the mount of congregation, **I** will ascend above the heights of the clouds; **I** will be like the most High" *(See Isaiah 14:12-15).* **I, I, I, the invincibility of I. I** (Edward) soon realized that **I** had fallen, become shattered, cut down, weakened to my knees in my own hell-the County Jail, a place where there was nothing **I** could do. I was placed in a pit for 12 days here my only task was to hear God. It was during this time, X-Men, that **I** realized that when you get **"I"** out of the way, you are in essence getting pride and the devil out of your life, so Christ can move in. X-Man is a Christ-Man; no longer **"I"** but Christ who lives in me.

God had cut me down with the very system I thought I could manipulate and control. My faith needed to be proven genuine (*see 1 Peter 1:7 and Hebrew 13:5*). Christ let me know I was going to do things His way or else. "The Lord of hosts hath sworn, saying, surely as I have thought, so shall it come to pass; and as I have purposed, so shall it stand" *(Isaiah 14:24).* I was in my valley experience, at my midnight hour and the only hand that was stretched out that could help was Jesus'. I was not about to turn His hand away. I submitted to Him and quickly learned how to be meek and humble. Before that time, I had always felt I could not pray. I was considered sophisticated and educated with an extensive vocabulary. I was known to be methodical, organized, unequivocating and thorough. But when it came to prayer, the devil had convinced me that I was unqualified and could never find the right words. But with this experience when I could do nothing, I learned how to pray and come into the presence of God. I learned to cast all my cares on the Lord and thank Him in faith for answering my prayers *(1 Peter 5:7)*. I learned to agree in prayer with other believers and to pray for my enemies, people whom I disliked and those who had mistreated or were currently mistreating me. I learned how to repent and forgive. My prayer for my partner is that one day he will die before he die. After all my years of faking and shaking, finally I wanted complete salvation. I wanted to walk the Christian walk and talk the Christian talk. I was willing to pay whatever price God required. I had forgotten that Jesus had paid the price for my salvation on Calvary. He put me in a position where I could not run and my personal skills were useless—all for the sake of making me humbled and qualified for service. As I write this book I can truly say He has taken me from Brookhaven to Broken to Beacon.

For the previous 12 years, I had been running like Jonah but now I was learning how to pray like Jonah. "Then Jonah prayed unto the Lord his God out of the fish's belly, and said, I cried by reason of mine affliction unto the Lord, and he heard me; out of the belly of hell cried I, and thou heardest my voice. For thou hadst cast me into the deep, in the midst of the seas; and the floods compassed me about: all thy billows and thy waves passed over me. Then I said, I am cast out of thy sight; yet I will look again toward thy holy temple. The waters compassed me about, even to the soul: the depth closed me round about; the weeds were wrapped about my head. I went down to the bottoms of the mountains; the earth with her bars was about me for ever: yet hast thou brought up my life from corruption, O Lord my God. When my soul fainted within me I remembered the Lord: and my prayer came in unto thee, into thine holy temple" *(Jonah 2:1-7)*. This prayer could have easily been mine, the only difference was time and location. I am so thankful that God heard my cry and brought me out. "He brought me up out of a horrible pit, out of the miry clay, and set my feet upon a rock, and established my goings" *(Psalms 40:2)*. X-Men, aren't you glad that God brought you out of your sins?

While incarcerated, I had felt like Bartimaeus trying to receive his sight. Despite the crowd, when Bartimaeus heard that Jesus was coming through town he cried out "Jesus thou son of David, have mercy on me!" Even though he was scorned and rebuked by a crowd of unbelievers, he continued to cry out. Because of his faith in Jesus, he received his sight *(Luke 18:35-42)*. I was in the first stage of my transformation and I was crying out. I wanted my salvation to be certain. I realized I was spiritually blind and like Bartimateus I was screaming out to the Lord for my sight. X-Men I do not know what is stopping you from seeing Jesus. Nevertheless, this one thing I know if you scream out to Jesus in spite of the crowd, He is able to grant what you ask.

Remember, during your qualifying experience, as you cry out God will meet you and all the Angles in heaven and all the X-Men will celebrate and be glad for you: "my Brother was dead and is alive again, was lost and is found." Before that October 21st day, I thought I was doing alright. I thought I was on my way. I had already accepted Christ as my savior; I had already confessed and accepted my calling into Ministry. But a proud man I was and like Hosea, a CCE course was needed. I felt like Hosea when he underwent his humbling experience, after already being a prophet. At first I felt that this was something the devil did because of my walk with Christ. I later understood it as an opportunity for God to prepare me for the ministry I was about to embark upon. My sister Minister Luader Smith told me, "God won't let you go forward until your all is on the altar of sacrifice. Like Lot's wife, when God tells you don't look back, you should take him at his words. In order for God to begin to use me, God had to expose my shortcomings. God had to test me, just as He will you to see if you will love Him with all your heart. As an X-Man you have to humble yourself and place your all on the altar of sacrifice, die to it and leave it there.

X-Men, at some point in your life, God will humble you by putting you in a position where you can hear and trust Him. Pure trust and faith in God only happens in places where only God can deliver you. If you are going to finish strong and not get stuck on third base, you can not go through life on cruise control. You can not get stuck on third base when you can see home plate. To get stuck on third base is worse than striking out, fouling out or never even getting up to bat. You are an X-Man now, qualified for battle. You are a soldier for Christ and we are at war. War has a way of testing our belief, our unity and our character. War can be both hell and glory. However, in order to obtain a major victory you have to sustain some small humbling losses. Just like the X-Men in the Marvel comics, X-Men for Christ are in a battle to save mankind. What man does not want to save the world in some form or another? Our foe, Satan thinks he is smarter and wiser than we are, simply because he has had more time to prepare. But in the midst of doubt and collapse of creed, remember that Christ shall always be more for us than the whole world against us. He will never leave you nor will He forsake you.

On the ninth day of incarceration I had been fasting and praying, trying to stay focused because I had been locked up longer than I had anticipated. I was originally supposed to be released on that Monday, but the Judge demanded that I be held until all the facts could be ascertained. He did not care who I was or what arrangements had been worked out. I was standing before the Judge to respond to allegations about a business deal gone bad where it was my partner word against mine. Unfortunately for me at the time, my partner had a better relationship with the District Attorney's office than I did. I wondered, "why now?" Why not two years ago when the incident actually took place? Even though I felt I was right in my actions toward my partners, I had been willing to not fight but to simply pay the disputed funds to the Court. I had been willing to pay my own way to appear in Court. There were correctional officers who were willing to escort me personally to Court if necessary. I was upset and felt that God had forgotten about me or had left me to teach me a lesson. But then *I* remembered that it was no longer *I* but Christ. I prayed fervently to God first for forgiveness. I told Him, "Lord I need you to show your self-strong today. I need to know that you are with me". Not too long after my prayer, the correctional officer called and said Edward you have a visitor. I was not expecting anyone, but I got prepared for my visit. When I walked into the visiting room, it was one of my good friends who had come share a word about humility and assured me that everything was going to be alright. In fact he stated that he would not be surprised if someone came for me that same day. At about 11:30 P.M. that night I was sitting in my cell reading when the Correctional officer came to my cell and said "Pack up! Someone is here to pick you up".

I thought I was making a straight trip to the Court House, which I thought would be the end of my qualifying experience, but boy was *I* wrong. God allowed me to travel two days and spend three more days in various jails. While waiting to get to Court, I was told that it could be several weeks before the matter was completed. I begin to become discouraged again, but I never quit praying to God. I told God my family did not know where I was and I had not talked to my children. I knew at that point that my family was worried, because no one knew where I was. I needed God to show Himself strong. I needed to know that He was still with me and that He had not forgotten about me. While I sat there in the holding cell holding back tears, the biggest guy in the cell sat down in front of me. While everyone else in the cell had on the same attire, his orange jump suit read "Christian County Jail" Christian, Kentucky. Seeing the guy in his jump suit was enough to give me hope. That single moment of triumph pushed me to want to hold on and see what new lesson God had for me. It was at that moment God was speaking to me and letting me know that even in Jail I was required to be a faithful Christian. He was letting me know that He was qualifying and justifying me. God was letting me know that I had been running from him for twelve years and it was time He got my attention so I could be used to uplift His kingdom. I had a new mission in life, and that was to be a member of His X-Men and to spend the rest of my natural life recruiting more X-Men to come to the Well and get a drink of water. Those inmates I was able to witness to, it was necessary for me to plant a seed in their lives. On the twelfth day of being locked up, the correctional officers picked me up to take me before the Judge for what would be the end of my twelve-step qualifying program. X-Men, if you are caught up in a situation, maybe you need to pray to God to show Himself. Maybe you are in a state of depression pray to God to show himself strong. If you are suffering from an illness, pray to God to show himself strong. Maybe you are trying to overcome an addiction, pray to God to show himself strong. Whatever the world has you caught up in, pray to God to show himself strong!

I now know a little something about meekness, humility and determination. I now understand what it means to surrender and bury your pride and past. Because of my experience, while in Jail, during my weakest hour I expressed strength under control. I found myself reaching out to other inmates, having bible studies and trying to share the word of God. I was not going to let the woman at the Well out do me. Even on the bus trips between jails, I found myself witnessing to other inmates and correction officers that if God could save me he could do a work in them. Through my pain of knowing what God had brought me through, I was able to witness to men in my cell that, Jesus saves and all they had to do was confess and forsake their sins. I needed them to understand, just like I need you to understand, that your past does not disqualify you from service with God. Know that when you are in the middle of a storm, be patient and pray; before you know it, the storm will die down and a rainbow will appear. God will give you peace in the midst of the storm.

When I think about being trapped and locked up, I think about Otis on the Andy Griffith show. He was considered the town drunk. I have had a few alcoholics in my family, so I know a little bit about intoxication and sobering up. Every time Otis got drunk he would go to the Sheriff's station and lock himself up in a cell. When he sobered up, he would let himself out of the cell, because Andy and Barney always left the cell unlocked or the key was always close by. I was locked up until I finally wisened-up and my spirit became sober from sin. X-Men, go into your tomorrow knowing that the cell is unlocked. Go into tomorrow knowing that Jesus has paid your bail. Go into tomorrow knowing your spirit can sober up. Go into tomorrow with no regrets. Like Paul and Silas, God will make the earth shake and chains break. If you ever get caught up-know that the doors of the church are always open and you can go and stay at the altar until your spirit is sober.

So after twelve years of running from my calling, God had taken twelve days to remake me, to get my attention, and He qualified me by letting me know that He was the one in control. On the 21st day of October (which is the reverse of the number 12), He started a chain of events that would send me backwards, in order that I might move forward. For twelve years, or 144 months, I had been running away. Twelve years or 624 weeks I separated myself from my calling and from God. For twelve years I had refused to press toward the mark. For twelve years, I epitomized the prodigal son's lifestyle before he lost everything and came to himself. For twelve years after knowing better, I had continued lost in my sins. Hopefully, you can now understand why I felt like Lazarus being called out of the tomb. I came out of jail and I knew that God had qualified me. He was now my Jehovah Jireh, my Jehovah Rapha; God had made me seek Him out so He could clothe me with His righteousness, stabilize me in truth, and strengthen me with authority. In my darkest hour, He came and showed Himself strong. Have you had a Lazarus experience? My twelve days of waiting and relying only on Christ forced me to recognize that *I* was not in control and it humbled me the way I needed to be humbled. On the twelfth day, I knew I had become a resurrected, qualified man. I was an X-Man. I was buried in jail for twelve days and when I was called out, I came out alive and born again. I came out like Apostle Paul. Paul endured greatly. Snakes bit him. Pagans, Jews and false Christians, expelled and persecuted him. He was whipped and thrown in jail, and he died everyday. His adversaries thought they had frightened him, humiliated him and decimated him, yet he exited jail refreshed, renewed, and reassured. Paul stated in *Romans 8:38-39* "I am persuaded that neither death nor life [. . . ,] neither the present nor the future, neither heights nor depth, nor other creatures, will be able to separate me from the love of God that is in Christ Jesus." I came out from behind those bars with a thanksgiving spirit, knowing my mission for my life and for my family. I was not thankful, because I had gotten away with doing wrong, but rather because I now understood God's master plan for my life my role in my church and in my community. I had tasted the Living Water. I had become qualified and I knew it was time to start inviting some people to the Well.

> *God give us men. A time like this demands Strong minds, great hearts, true faith and ready hands. Men whom the lust of office does not kill. Men whom the spoils of office cannot buy. Men who possess opinions and a will, Men who love honor, men who will not lie.*
>
> *Josiah Gilbert Holland*

INTERLUDE

The Power Of Twelve—A Prophetic Number

Before going to the next session, I have to pause here to include an observation that was brought to my attention by my wife, Aisha. She asked me a very important question that required understanding, an explanation and some appreciation. She asked me how I knew when I had first heard from God and started running. Secondly, she asked me if there was anything significant about the number 12 and my qualifying experience. When you consider the twelve years I spent running, the twelve days I spent in chains and twelve sessions of this book, you at least have to ponder the thought. Even though there was something strange about it, I had not before then thought to give the number 12 much consideration.

As I contemplated the issue, I began to notice and recall the frequency of times the number had manifested in my life, and realized it had been an underlying constant in my life. As I reflected further, I realized that I am the youngest of twelve children. My siblings were: Abdullah, Helen, Margaretta, Bobby Joe, Brenda, Shirley, Wallace, Luader, Laura, R.W. Benson, Jr., Diane. (I always had to count on my fingers and list them just to make sure). I remembered I was twelve years old when people started predicting that one day I would become a pastor. I did not know much about prophecy at the time, but my work in the church was becoming more visible. We had a small congregation at First Temple Church of Christ Holiness U.S.A. (also known in the Brookhaven community as "Spot without a Wrinkle") so participation by everyone was important. I started teaching Sunday School and serving as Junior Deacon. I began to emulate our Pastor, Reverend Tate. I would often be asked to sing one of his favorite songs as a solo at the various churches we attended. Songs like the, "the King is Coming", "He Touched Me" and "How Great Thou Art" were among his favorites. Even at the age of twelve, God was using me and calling me to come home. I just didn't know it at the time. I now recall that Jesus himself was twelve when He first spoke in the temple.

Twelve years later I found myself in my first year of Law School, and that was also the year my daughter was born. I was sitting in a Christian Legal Society meeting and a Minister whose name I don't recall was the guest speaker. He asked if we knew the Supreme Being Jesus Christ, I realized that I had known of him all my life, but I didn't really know him. I remember thinking it was belittling for the

Minister to read a children's book titled "Just in case you ever Wonder" to a group of law students. Yet, his words began to convict me that I really did not belong in Law School, that Christ had another calling on my life, but I wasn't hearing it. I was so convicted that I purchased the book and would often read it to my daughter as a bed-time story. Even though I was walking outside of God's will, I wanted so much for her to know about God's love and that He would always be there for her. I subsequently read the same book to my other children, because I wanted them to know Christ early in life. Even though I was refusing to walk in my calling, little did I understand God was teaching me that He would always be there, just in case I ever wondered.

God was calling me into Ministry. I knew of all the prophecies on my life, made by my grandfather, Reverend Hillary Edwards, my Pastor, Reverend C. D. Tate, my birth mother, Evangelist Glossie Edwards, my beloved step-mother Beulah Benson, my Aunt, Mary Jane Dillon and other Christians. He was calling me into Ministry and out of Law School, and although I could hear Him as clearly as a bell, I would not listen. All I could think about was what would the community think?" My dad used to say, "damn the people, they don't have a heaven or hell to put you in!" That's one piece of advice from my dad I should have taken to heart. I had always wanted to be a Lawyer and never a minister. Everyone in Brookhaven knew I was in Law School and I could not quit. I was the talk of the community and I wanted to make everybody proud, except God. The pride of life had me and I did not even know it. In Fourth grade my teacher once asked me what I wanted to be when I grew up. I assuredly and proudly replied, "a Lawyer". I wanted to be a lawyer simply because I thought it was impressive. I would often tell Reverend Tate whenever he brought up the subject, "I wouldn't have your job for nothing!" Nevertheless, I also told him and other pastors that if I ever started preaching, they would know it was a calling from God. The late Percy Dixon was one person who stayed on my case especially when he found out that I had quit singing in the church. He let me know that in the end only what I would do for Christ would last.

A Minister? Not me, I didn't think so. I didn't want to have to deal with people on that level. Sure, I could walk into court and defend someone's life, but I didn't want the responsibility of another's person's soul. I didn't want the responsibility of dealing with their attitudes, their problems or their faith. So I dismissed the notion every time someone would raise the question. I dismissed it and kept running away every time I was confronted. I ran like Jonah and hid for another twelve years. Well, God did not put me in the belly of a whale; instead He put me in jail for twelve days. Do you remember being young and someone asked what you wanted to become when you grew up? Do you recall your response? How often is it that when a person is asked that question, their reply would be, "I just want to grow up saved or I just want to work for the Lord."

So what is the significance of twelve, if any? What was the significance of my being the twelfth child, the twelve years I spent running, twelve days in jail and now these twelve sessions on X-Men? Was it of any significance that my favorite shortcut exit home was Exit 12 on the main intersection I-84 (8+4=12)? The meeting I had scheduled for October 21st day was originally scheduled for 11:00 A.M., but then it was moved back for convenience to 12:00 Noon. The change in schedule that sparked my high noon, midnight experience. I was seeing the number 12 everywhere and it was confirmation of my calling. I tell you, after doing a little research on the subject of twelve, I was shocked by the biblical revelation. I was shocked that the number was not coincidental but ordained by God. I found that the number twelve spiritually points to the congregation of God; twelve brothers, the twelve sons of Jacob who were the progenitors of the twelve tribes of Israel and the twelve apostles who dropped their lifestyles and followed Jesus: why the number twelve is so important in the kingdom. *Rev. 21:12, 14* "And had a wall great and high and had twelve gates, and at the gates twelve angels, and names written thereon, which are the names of the Twelve Tribes of the Children of Israel:" [. . .] "And the wall of the city had twelve foundations, and in them the names of the Twelve Apostles of the lamb." The city measured twelve thousand furlongs, having twelve precious stones. When Jesus fed the 5000 at the largest fish fry ever, there was twelve fragments of food left over. The damsel Jesus arose from the dead was twelve years old. I too had been resurrected after twelve years. I too had now dropped everything to follow Christ. I too was now blessed with a new foundation of a new ministry birth in my heart by Christ. I too had started the race that would allow me on Judgment day to enter into one of the twelve gates.

The number 12 has been used throughout the bible to signify unity and completeness: the 12 pillars set up by Moses in *Exodus 24:14*; the 12 jewels in the high priest's breast plate in *Exodus 28:21*; the 12 officers appointed by Solomon in *1 Kings 4:7*; the 12 stones of Elijah's altar in *1 Kings 18:31;* the 12 cakes of showbread in the temple found in *Leviticus 24:5*; the 12 rods mentioned in Numbers 17:2 or the 12 spies Moses sent to spy on the land of Canaan in *Numbers chapter 13*; the 12 stones placed by Joshua in the bed of Jordan in *Joshua 4:9.*

The number 12 when reduced in numerology as 1+2 = 3 becomes symbolic of the trinity. Now, at the age of thirty-six, the circle of my life has gone around three times, "my third Anniversary of twelve." The number three is used by God to signify His Purpose or His Will. In *1 King 17:21* Elijah shadowed his body over a dead child three times, and the child lived again. Jesus rose from the dead after three days. I had experienced three intervals of twelve. On my first anniversary of twelve, God called me into ministry, calling me for His purpose, to do his will. On my second anniversary, He called me out of Law School and I began to flee from Him. On my third Anniversary, He locked me up, held me still and said "enough is enough". Three times twelve (3 X 12) it took Jesus to get my attention, one for the Father, one for the Son and one for the Holy Ghost. I had survived the midnight, now it was Show-Down at high noon, twelve o'clock and Jesus was calling me out.

After my twelve days in jail and the extra week I spent working things out—I had come back home, to learn I had lost my job. I was unemployed and attended interviews for about three weeks. Almost three months later after that October experience, I was finally blessed with a job as a recruiter. My start date was December 12th. That's right, the twelfth month on the twelfth day. The X-Man recruiter was now also employed as a recruiter. I figured God wanted to give me some practical experience to prepare me as a recruiter of X-Men. I got to read some impressive resumes, but none was as impressive as the Resume of Jesus Christ. I had reviewed Christ's resume in detail and concluded he was more qualified than I to be the head of my life.

When the soldiers came to get Jesus after He was betrayed by Judas, switchblade totting Disciple Peter wanted to fight. Jesus stated, "Thinkest thou that I cannot now pray to My Father, and he shall presently give me more than twelve Legions of Angels? Jesus referred to His army that would do battle for Him as twelve Legions. He could have said eleven, but he said twelve. He could have brought me out in one day, but he took twelve. I could have accepted my calling in one year, but it took me twelve. When I went to the first Bible study for "Men Only" at Springfield, the total number of students in attendance was twelve. I now understand that I to am now in the army of the Lord. I now understand that my twelve years, twelve days and the numerous hours I spent arguing cases before juries of twelve was no accident, rather it was preparation for a higher calling. If you are a recovering alcoholic, I submit, it is no accident that the road to recovery is a twelve step program. I have a sister who was an alcoholic and she taught me that you can't fix what you are not willing to face. When I look at where she was and where the Lord has brought her, I am inspired.

I returned to Court on February 21, 2006 to finalize matters that surrounded my October 21, 2005 encounter. I realized that there was that 2 and 1 again, the reverse of 12. I now understand that although it was Highway 84 (8+4=12) in Brookhaven, it, like me was running in the wrong direction. The day when I finally stood before the Judge, I was worried whether anyone was going to be able to look past the obvious and see the real facts. I was trusting in God as to who He would use as His instrument, and behold it was the Judge who was both understanding and compassionate. When he saw my dilemma, he went out of his way to accommodate my situation. As I sat there and watched things unfold, I realized that God had a front row seat interceding on my behalf in the form of the Judge himself. When everything was said and done, I found myself sitting at a Bible study. As I wrote down the date on my offering envelope, I again realized that the number 12 had surfaced. It was February 22, 2006 or 2/22/06 and all numbers added together equaled 12. I was finally putting some closure to my past and God had granted me an opportunity to move on. I had been made righteous and complete by the virtue of Jesus.

God meticulously pointed out and reminded me that the woman with an issue of blood suffered twelve years before she was made righteous by Jesus Christ. No one, no physician she saw could heal her. It took only the virtue of Jesus. After all I went through it was worth it all to be saved and justified by the virtue of Christ. I pray continuously and thank God for you X-Men who will come to Christ willingly, for I myself came to Him in chains.

SESSION NINE

Overcoming The Struggles Of Life

"Life is easy, living is Hard"

LIFE'S STRUGGLES

Life can seem ungrateful and not always kind.
Life can pull at your heartstrings and play with your mind
Life can be blissful and happy and free
Life can put beauty in the things that you see
Life can place challenges right at your feet
Life can make good of the hardships we meet
Life can overwhelm you and make your head spin
Life can reward those determined to win
Life can be hurtful and not always fair
Life can surround you with people who care
Life clearly does offer its Up and its Downs
Life's days can bring you both smiles and frowns
Life teaches us to take the good with the bad
Life is a mixture of happy and sad
So
Take the Life you have and give it your best
Think positive; be happy let God do the rest
Take the challenges that life has laid at your feet
Take pride and be thankful for each one you meet
To yourself give forgiveness if you stumble and fall
Take each day that is dealt you and give it your all
Take the love that you're given and return it with care
Have faith that when needed it will always be there
Take time to find the beauty in the things that you see
Take life's simple pleasures let them set your heart free
The idea here is simply to even the score
As you are met and faced with Life's tug of War
by Heart and Soul Group

O.K., let's take the testimonial music off pause and push play as we move this transformation forward. X-Men now that you've received your justification and qualification, and you have prayed, confessed and repented of your prideful nature and learned to be submissive, meek and humble, don't think that life will simply get easier. I once heard "life is not a journey to the grave with the intention of arriving safely in a pretty and well preserved body, but rather to skid in broadside, thoroughly used up, totally worn out, and loudly proclaiming—WOW, what a ride!" I know life can get hard sometimes, but you need to remember who you are and whose you are. X-Man, you are a royal priesthood. When your life in Christ has come full circle and you sincerely trust and depend on Him, He will be your Jehovah-Tsidkenu, your righteousness; Jehovah-Shammah, ever present with you; Jehovah-Nissi, your banner; Jehovah-Rahi, your loving Shepard; Jehovah-Rophe, your healer; Jehovah-Jireh; your provider; Jehovah m'Kaddesh, your sanctification; and Jehovah-Shalom, your peace. When you are tempted by Satan, you can look to Jesus from whom your help comes. You can stand boldly and confess to yourself, "I can't give up I've come too far to turn around. I've passed the point of no return. I am in the midst of my transformation. I am a new anointed creature in Christ, old things have passed away." However, as you confess, be realistic about your past and realize that not everyone will cheer when you get back up after a fall and follow Christ. But when you are confronted concerning the man you were, you stand boldly and proclaim the man you have become. Tell them that you are an X-Man, a New Creature, who by the grace and power of Jesus Christ come to recruit and draw other sinners to Him who can save their souls. Tell them the old you is dead and buried.

1 John 5:3-6 "For this is the love of God, that we (X-Men) keep His commandments. And His commandments are not burdensome. For whatever is born of God overcomes the world. And this is the victory that has overcome the world-our faith. Who is he (X-Men) who overcomes the world, but he (X-Men) who believes that Jesus is the Son of God?" Every man in the Church is an X-something, so do not get discouraged, be of good cheer, for Christ has overcome the world. Your past mistakes are stepping stone not stumbling blocks. Think about the things that you have already overcome in your life. Think of the things you struggled with that you thought you would never survive. Remember, with God's grace, you made it through. Do not live a life of conviction and regret for one or even a hundred mistakes. Don't let your legacy be based on society's unwillingness to forgive and forget. History reminds me that when President McKinley was shot, he was attended by two physicians, Dr. Weiss and Dr. Bliss. Since X-rays had not yet been invented, the doctors could only guess where the bullet was. They followed Dr. Bliss, opinion but Dr. Bliss was wrong. President McKinley died. The next day, the newspapers headline read "Ignorance is Bliss!" X-Man, don't let the ignorance of the world hold you in captivity, by their refusal to forget your pass mistakes. The last prayer Jesus said was one of forgiveness of our ignorance. "Father forgive them, for they know not what they do"(*Luke 23:34*). So you made a few mistakes, Jesus forgives you and He has given you the strength to overcome.

Acts 4:12 states "Nor is there salvation in any other for there is no other name under heaven given among men by which we must be saved." X-Man, we are over comers because Jesus overcame the world and died for our sins. What can wash away my sins? . . . Nothing but the blood of Jesus! It doesn't matter what you were; you can take up the cross of Christ and *X* it out of your life. It does not matter what condition you were in yesterday you can walk for Christ today. In *Acts 4:14* and 22 we read "And seeing the (X-man) who had been healed standing with them, they could say nothing against it. *Acts 4:22* For the man was over forty years old on whom this miracle of healing had been performed." When men see the miracle of grace in your life they will look at you in amazement and disbelief saying nothing against you. If you are sick, God can heal you. X-Man it is time you got up and stood erect and walked like the man of God you are. If you need inspiration to overcome just look around or look in the bible there are numerous men and women who have overcome. Look at Mary Magdalene who was recorded in the Bible of as a repentant prostitute. Nevertheless scripture teaches us that after her repentance she found favor and great praise in the eyes of God. She went from being a prostitute to being an X-prostitute.

Consider the life of Zacchaeus who was a thief camouflaged as a tax collector. *Luke 19:1* testifies that Zacchaeus was a wealthy man. Obviously, he was good at his job. When Jesus came to Jericho, Zacchaeus wanted to see Him. Because he was short in statute, Zacchaeus first tried to run to try to get ahead of the crowd to see Jesus, to no avail. When all else failed, he ultimately climbed a sycamore tree to get a good view of his Savior. Although Jesus had never met him, Jesus called him by name. Jesus saw past Zacchaeus's crimes into his heart and offered him forgiveness, mercy and acceptance. Zacchaeus subsequently chose Jesus over his wealth. What he had to give up was nothing compared to what he was gaining in Jesus. How clear is your choice? X-Man, although Jesus has never met you, He is calling you by name.

X-Men are over comers because they are doers of the word. *James 1:22-25* tells us, "But be ye doers of the word, and not hearers only, deceiving your own selves. For if any be a hearer of the word, and not a doer, he is like unto a man beholding his natural face in a glass: for he behold himself, and goeth his way, and straight-way fretted what manner of man he was. But whoso looketh into the perfect law of liberty, and continueth therein, he being not a forgetful hearer, but a doer of the work, this man shall be blessed in his deed." X-Man, God is watching your every move and wants to order your every step. Living and bearing the burdens of life can be made easier by allowing God to order your steps.

As the song goes, "Jesus is a rock in a weary land." However sometimes the only way for a man to learn the true spirit of a rock is to stub his toe on it. X-Men are doers and overcomers. I often realize that most men feel that there is something in their life that they cannot overcome. It seems that even though you are focused on doing what is right you find yourself slipping back picking up bad habits and making bad decisions. X-Man it is alright to fall short or even fail, but it is never alright to quit. You simply need to remember that He is faithful and just to forgive your every bad moment, bad habit, selfish mood, white lie, every flop and every failure. Remember you are an X-Man, your father is the King of Kings and Lord of Lords, He is a present help in the time of trouble, give it to Jesus and let Him handle it. He will stick closer to you than any brother for He will never leave you nor forsake you.

> *DON'T BE AFRAID TO FAIL: You've failed many times, although you may not remember. You fell down the first time you tried to walk. You almost drowned the first time you tried to swim, didn't you? Did you hit the ball the first time you swung the bat? Heavy Hitters, the ones who hit the most home runs also strike out a lot. R. H. Macy failed seven times before his store in New York caught on. English novelist John Creasey got 753 rejection slips before he published 564 books. Babe Ruth struck out 1,330 times, but he also hit 714 Home Runs. Don't worry about failures, worry about the chances you miss when you don't even try.*

> *Author Unknown*

Most people think Peter failed a very important test of faith when, as he was walking on the water, he took his eyes off of Christ and begin to sink. However, I submit the true failures were the other eleven disciples who were afraid to get off the boat. He who has never failed cannot be great. Failure is the true test of greatness. A just man falleth seven times, but what makes him just is that each time he falls he gets back up again. An X-Man is a just man justified by God. If you have fallen get back up again and keep running, harder and faster. If you are sinking don't worry, God will reach down and save you. You will look around and realize you are having a WOW experience (Walking ON Water experience). Instead of running away from God, now is the time to start running for Him and with Him.

Remember whatever you are dealing with, you are neither alone nor are you without hope. Whatever you do, do not let fleshly opinion and earthly circumstances hinder your pursuit of God. Do not let society's murmuring delay your progress. Remember everyone fails, but you're only a failure if you refuse to learn from your mistakes or if you quit. X-Men must have a teachable spirit and learn from past mistakes and move past any shame. So what if we live in a world that is fast moving and unforgiving. *Hebrew 12:1-2* reads, "wherefore seeing we also are compassed about with so great a cloud of witnesses, let us lay aside every weight, and the sin which doth so easily beset us, and let us run with patience the race that is set before us, Looking unto Jesus the author and finisher of our faith; who for the joy that was set before him endured the cross, despising the shame, and is set down at the right hand of the throne of God."

I know sometimes we experience setbacks in life. I know you may have been disappointed by family or friends. Maybe you have been despised and shamed. I know you may feel that there is no way out. But I assure you if you just hold on and don't quit, God will pull you through. Just like God dealt with Moses after Moses had killed the Egyptian, He is not finished dealing with you. God transformed a murderer into a deliverer of a nation. Can you imagine what He can do for you? It took God forty (40) years to equip Moses for his calling and his destiny. Abraham waited 99 years for his promise. If you feel God has forgotten about you—he hasn't. Everything you have lost, everything you are experiencing is in preparation for your destiny as an X-Man. I know you have been caused to suffer, but it is the suffering that is qualifying you for ministry. Before God can use you He has to break you and rebuild you. Isn't it time you were broken?

X-Man, I know you are excited about your ministry, but don't rush your calling or get impatient with God. But I say wait upon the Lord and he shall renew your strength. God hasn't abandoned the dream He placed in your heart. You may not know how you are going to get there from where you are, but He knows. Where you are now is not where God is taking you. Remember when Joseph was sold into slavery and placed in the pit and later in prison. He couldn't see the road to the palace, but God knew exactly where he was taking Joseph and He knows exactly where He is taking you. He is evolving your spirit. In case you didn't notice transformation takes time.

SESSION TEN

"Do You Believe In Superman?"

A Man With A Calling?

As a child, one of my favorite super heroes was Superman. I would become filled with excitement and anticipation as the TV extras would point up to the sky and shout: "it's a bird, it's a plane. No, its Superman!" They knew that their hero had come to save the day. Well, I no longer believe in the man of steel from the planet Krypton, but I do believe in Superman. I believe in a baby from heaven born in Bethlehem, not some fictional character growing up in Smallville, Kansas. I don't believe in a man of steel camouflaging as a news reporter for the Daily Planet in Metropolis. I do believe in a mild mannered easy-going Savior. I believe in a soft-spoken miracle worker. I believe in a good-natured Deliver who walked on earth over 2000 years ago and humbled Himself as a carpenter from Nazareth. Why should I care about or be scared of a so-called villainous genius archenemy named Lex Luthor (Lucifer)? Especially, when I know a man who is more powerful than Satan and all his demons. Someone who is mightier than Katrina, the roaring hurricane that hit the shores of the Gulf Coast. He is faster than the speeding bullets that could have taken my life years ago. I am still amazed how He leaps over all of my life-size tribulations with a single bound. He has proven to be more powerful than death and the grave. X-Man, I believe in Superman. In fact I'm a **Super-Fan** of Superman. My Superman, the Savior that no kryptonite could harm. A Savior whose act of giving up His life and shedding His blood was so heroic, it changed the way we viewed time it self-as being either before his birth or after His death. **(B.C or A.D.).** A Superman who was resurrected as the most powerful man on earth and in heaven. X-Man, as you walk in your calling, look up in the sky, cause our Superman will one day burst through the heavens, to call His children home. When you are faced with trials and tribulations, look up in the sky, for Jesus will come and save the day.

I confess, I do not know what God has in store for you, other than a life of service to Him. I understand that each of us at some point has been filled with the illusion that we must assume the role of hero as we progress from boyhood to manhood to fatherhood. I agree that it is imperative that you grasp the view or philosophy of

becoming and surviving as a man, so you can adequately convey to your children what you stand for and what you are willing to die for. It is without question that you must develop your identity as a person and as a Christian by learning the difference between success as a man and fulfillment as an X-Man. It is time for you to grow into maturity and self-purpose by finding your calling.

How do you find your calling? Maybe you are aware of your calling, yet you have been running. Maybe you know your calling but feel unqualified, thus wavering in your faith. Maybe you know, but facing road blocks. Maybe you feel you do not have the time or resources needed to devote to your calling. Maybe it will mean a loss or decrease in income. Maybe you feel you will disappoint family or become unpopular with friends. Whatever, your thinking, X-Man, pray about your calling daily. X-Man pray. The bible does not demand that X-Men always ought to go to church. It does not suggest that X-Men should sing in the choir. It doesn't allude to the fact that one should join the usher board, trustee board, deacon board, or to teach bible study or Sunday school class. However, it clearly states that X-Men always ought to pray and not lose heart(*See Luke 18:1*). X-Man, always does not means sometimes but all the time. *1 Thessalonians 5:17*, tells us to "Pray without ceasing." When you put the two verses together, you will see that there are times to pray briefly and times to pray at length. There is a time and place for corporate prayer and then there are times you need lift up a quick word and receive a quick answer. While standing on the Red Sea, Moses momentarily hesitated to pray to God for the pursuing Egyptians. Sometimes brothers, you got to **drop it like it's hot**—but pray. If God has called you into ministry, you need to have a hotline. If you are still trying to find your way, don't just sit gazing in the clouds—pray.

It took me twelve years and twelve days, but now I'm certain what His plans are for me. I even know what I desire for myself. His desire for me is the one thing I desire more than life. It is the one thing that keeps me going and holding on. It is the one thing that makes me want to ring the bell everyday and fight one more round. It is the one thing that won't let me quit: the desire to recruit new X-men and women. I press forward because I desire to hear Him call my name and say "Edward, your living was not in vain: well done my good and faithful servant."

Now that you are an overcomer AND YOU KNOW God can use you, seek HIM for your calling. Do you know why God called you to be one of his X-Men? In *Ephesians 4:1-2; 4* we read "I (Paul), therefore, the prisoner of the Lord, beseech you (X-Men) to walk worthy of the calling with which you were called. With all lowliness and gentleness, with longsuffering, bearing with one another in love [. . .] there is one body and one Spirit, just as you (X-Men) were called in one hope of your calling," After all that God has done for you, don't you want to know your calling? Don't you want to use your gift and let your life have an eternal meaning? Don't you want to be able to respond to the Nay—Sayers and tell them that a hero lives inside of you? Tell them you are now an X-Man, a New Creature who by the grace and power of Christ has come to recruit and draw sinners to Him who can save their soul? Tell them you know Superman.

Understand that your call to Ministry does not necessarily mean that God has called you to the Pulpit. Ministry could be anywhere that you can serve God. If you are a Christian, you are in full time ministry. According to *Ephesians 4:11-13* and *Colossians 3:23* the fact that you don't collect a paycheck for your service is irrelevant. I don't care what you do for a living, if you know Jesus Christ as Lord and Savior, essentially, you already work for Him. Jesus said you are the light of the world. He said you are the salt of the Earth and He didn't say anything about the job being part-time. Your new calling is magnificent, spectacular, and Godly ordained by God to exceed your wildest dreams. It is time for you to be the person you were meant to be, an X-Man, and everything else will follow. Seek ye first the kingdom of God and all of His righteousness and all these things will be added unto you. Remember you didn't choose God, God chose you. God is looking for a few good men. In reference to destroying Sodom, God told Abraham if he could walk through the city and find ten good men, that city would be saved. It is disheartening to think that God could ask the same of some of our Pastors today and they would not even be able to find ten good men in some of our churches.

God has been waiting on you to accept your calling. He has been waiting for you to pick up your cross and submit to Him as He submitted to the cross on Calvary. He has blessed you with many gifts and He is requiring that you give back in the form of service. *Luke 12:48* says "For unto whomsoever much is given, of him shall be much required: and to whom men have committed much, of him they will ask the more." Your calling will cost you to endure, it will require longsuffering and despite your reservations it is your cross to bear. "If any man come to Me and hate not his own life, he cannot be My disciple. And whosoever doth not bear his cross, and come after Me, cannot be My disciple." *Luke 14:26-27*. When you come to Jesus he takes your *"X"* and turns it into a cross that only you can bear. Whether the insignia is viewed as an *X* or a *cross* depends solely on how you carry it.

In order to walk in your calling you have got to love God above all else. It is time for you to bear your cross (accept your calling). This cup will not pass from your lips. Christ prayed to His father to let the cup pass Him by. I can imagine, if his fleshly body had a say in the matter, whether He would have asked God to send someone else for the job. He would have inquired if there were another way or why God couldn't just continue to send His word through His priests. He would have said "Let Moses go back and die. Send Abraham, Isaac or Jacob. Send Adam back, maybe he'll get it right this time." But Jesus knew why He was born and what His calling. He was called to die for your sins and mine. God knew no one else could save the day, but Superman Jesus. Just like Jesus followed His calling, it is your calling to be a minister, deacon, teacher, trustee, evangelist, choir member, servant leader, etc. X-Man, God has a calling on your life: it is your cross to bear, so pick it up, embrace it and follow after Christ.

Your future is beyond prediction, other than the fact that one day you will surely die and God has a calling on your life. How many tomorrows will pass before you walk in your calling? How long will it be before you go to the Well for a drink of water? How long will it take for your transformation into a new creature? What if Hell is your only alternative after this life? God is calling you into service, pick up your cross and follow Him. Do not worry if your own family cannot see the calling God has on your life, for you have overcome. The bible say, "[He] made himself of no reputation" (*Philippians 2:7*). Jesus didn't care what other people thought of Him and neither should you.

God told Samuel to go to the house of Jesse to anoint a King. Although, Samuel was coming for dinner to anoint a king, Jesse did not think enough of his son David to even invite him. Although Jesse considered David to be obscure and did not recognize him, David had a calling on his life. When Samuel thought that the new King would be one of David's brothers, God told him, "Do not consider his appearance or his height, for I have rejected him." The Lord does not look at the things man looks at. Man looks at the outward appearance, but the Lord looks at the heart." (*1 Samuel 16:7*) Even today society does the same thing, we judge a book by its cover. How many times have you been judged by what people see? How many times has someone formed an opinion about you because of the way you dress, the way you wear your hair, the shoes you wear, the way you walk, the car you drive, how much money you have, the color of your skin, or the way you talk? How many times has someone looked at you and recognized God's calling in your life? How often do people see Superman in you? Although your family may have counted you out, God has not forgotten you. He has anointed you for a great work; He is waiting to put an **S** on your chest and call you Servant.

Your salvation is waiting for you. Won't you come home? If you are uncertain about your salvation, understand that Salvation does not come by confirmation. Your trip to heaven is not guaranteed by a confirmation number from Expedia. Salvation doesn't come by communion, baptism, church membership, and church attendance, trying to keep the Ten Commandments, or living out the Sermon on the Mount. It does not come by simply being moral and respectable, giving to charity, believing that there is a God or even claiming to be a Christian. Salvation comes only when we confess and receive in faith the gift of God's grace. Grace is the first and foremost provision of the gospel; it is neither earned nor deserved. We are all **charity cases**. Your appreciation for this great gift should be shown by accepting and walking in your calling.

When God called Jeremiah to preach to a people who would not listen, Jeremiah cried so much he became known as the weeping prophet. A call by God may not yield the worldly recognition you were expecting, such as in your career. A career is a chosen pursuit; a profession or occupation of one's working life. A Career is often how we define ourselves. Whereas a calling is an inner urge or a strong impulse, especially one believed to be divinely inspired to accept the Gospels as truth and Jesus as one's personal savior. A calling is how God defines our eternal life. A career is something you choose, something you do for yourself that ends with retirement. A calling is something you receive, something you do to glorify God that ends with death. For me my past career is over, but my calling has just begun. Accepting a calling means stepping out of your comfort zone. A calling causes God to use common people to do uncommon things. A calling requires us to sometimes walk in unfamiliar territory. A calling requires you to endure. Noah was 500 years old when he started to build the Ark which took 120 years to complete. A calling will require you to endure the rain to see the rainbow. X-Man, spend some time thinking about what a life without God will yield you verses a life with Him. Which one do you choose? When asked who my hero is, my response is, "Jesus—someone who is in touch with His emotions enough to cry at His friend's funeral, yet powerful enough to raise him from the dead." My hero is Superman Jesus. Who is your hero? Is your hero born of the divine birth of a virgin? Can your hero raise himself from the dead and hold all power in heaven and on earth in His hand? Can your hero walk on water or calm the sea? How strong is your hero? The bible states, "the name of Jesus is a strong tower, the righteous run to it and are safe" *(Proverbs 18:10)*. There is power in the name of Jesus.

Remember the man of steel could not raise the dead or walk on water, feed 5000, heal the lepers or make the blind see. The man of steel could not save Clark Kent, but thank God Christopher Reeves knew the real Superman. The man of steel did not transcend into the sky to build me a mansion on high. The man of steel may have had X-ray vision, but our Superman sits high and looks low, beholding the good and the bad. X-Man, when you are facing danger and stress beyond relief, remember you know Superman. Buddha may provide spiritual enlightment, but Jesus is the light of the world. Hinduism may have over 300,000 gods and goddesses, but Jesus is King of Kings and Lord of Lords. Remember Jesus is known as Alpha and Omega, the Shepherd and Bishop of Souls, the Chief Corner Stone, the Author and Finisher of Our Faith. There is no longer a need to debate Islamic or Muslim religion, Allah or the life of Muhammad, because X-Men know Superman.

They say the man of steel is stronger and faster than a locomotive. But we X-Men have assurance that our Superman Jesus made the entire Universe and holds it in the palm of His hand. We know that His name shall be called Wonderful, Counseller, The Mighty God, The Everlasting Father, The Prince of Peace (Isaiah 9:6).

In the words of Mariah Carey, "Lord know Dreams are hard to follow, But Don't let anyone Tear them away. Hold on There will be tomorrow, In time you'll find the way. And then a hero comes along with the strength to carry on And you cast your fears aside And you know you can survive. So when you feel like hope is gone, Look inside you and be strong And you'll finally see the truth That a hero (X-Man)lies in you."

Do not worry about the world making room for your calling, because they fell to see the hero in you. Remember before honor there is humility. "A man's gift maketh room for him, and bringeth him before great men." (*Proverbs 18:16*). X-Man, your time will come. You may have hurt some people along the way and made a mess of your life at times. You may have been decimated and demeaned by those who have attempted to control your destiny. You may have been considered an outcast, marginalized and rejected. You may have probably broken all ten commandments and everyone in your past may not be as excited about your calling as you are. Nevertheless, know that the same God who made Heaven and Earth and formed you in His image, in time, will require this world to make room for you. So search for the hero inside yourself. For Superman Jesus is the key to everlasting life and He lives inside of you.

SESSION ELEVEN

A Friend Like No Other

"A friend in need is a friend in deed"

A FRIEND

Standing by
All the way
Here to help you through your day
Holding you up
When you are weak
Helping you find what it is you seek.

Catching your tears
When you cry
Pulling you through when the tide is high.

Just being there, through thick and thin,
All just to say, you are my friend.
by: Brittani Kokko

Now that you are prepared to walk in your calling, if you haven't done so already, it is now time to find a friend. Friends are truthful, loyal, understanding, trustworthy and forgiving. A friend is someone with whom you can share your most intimate thoughts and feelings and who provides spiritual support. Recognize and embrace Superman Jesus as your friend. When I was yet a sinner, Jesus called me friend. "A friend loveth at all times, and a brother is born for adversity" (*Proverbs 17:17*). Jesus called His disciples not servants, but friends. In *John 15:14*, Jesus gives a clear-cut condition for being His friend: "ye are my friends, if ye do whatever I command you." The purpose of God's creation was that man would serve Him and be a representative of His character. The key to being a friend of Jesus is obedience. In fact, obedience is the standard for every relationship with Him. Picking up our cross is the most significant sign of obedience, for it involves nothing less than committing ourselves to do what God has called us to perform.

Friendship with Jesus is a fantastic privilege. X-Man next time you're in a group where someone is dropping the names of people they know, drop the name of Jesus. Tell them you're a personal friend of the Son of God. Tell them you know the Superman. In *John 15:12-16*, Jesus gives us five characteristics of his friends. His friends love each other, know His divine truth, are chosen out of this world (X-Men), bear visible fruit, and have their prayers answered. Webster's dictionary says that a friend is one who desires to entertain another's pleasure; one who holds another in high esteem, respect, and affection; a friend is one whose happiness and prosperity you desire to promote. To be a friend of Jesus means He holds you in esteem and promotes your happiness and prosperity. That's why He is sitting on the right hand of His Father constantly interceding on your behalf. X-Man, how does your friendship measure up?

When you are confronted with life's toils and strife, go to the one who can lift you from the depths of sins and shame. I pray you will go to Jesus; He should be your best friend. X-Man pray. Prayer is a conscious intent to have a heart to heart conversation with Christ. No X-Man is greater than his prayer life. Your effectual fervent prayers releases the dynamic power of Jesus Christ and solidifies your commitment and trust in God. When the solution to your problem lies beyond your abilities, X-Man pray to your friend. As Joseph Scriven and Charles C. Converse wrote in their renowed Baptist hymn:

> "*What a Friend We have in Jesus, all our sins and griefs to bear! What a privilege to carry Everything to God in prayer! O what peace we often forfeit, O what needless pain we bear, all because we do not carry Everything to God in prayer! Have we trials and temptations? Is ther trouble anywhere? We should never be discouraged-Take it to the Lord in prayer. Can we find a friend so faithful Who will all our sorrows share? Jesus knows our every weakness-Take it to the Lord in prayer. Are we weak and heavy laden, cumbered with a load of care? Precious Savior, still our refuge Take it to the Lord in prayer. So thy friends despise, for sake thee? Take it to the Lord in prayer. In His arms He'll take and shield thee-Thou wilt find a solace there.*"

Prayer is the basis of our Christian relationship. X-Man communicate with your friend Jesus by prayer. There is no greater blessing than to have a friend who always cares.

Just like Batman had Robin and Spiderman had his amazing friends, an X-Man needs to have a good friend in addition to Jesus. God recognized that even Adam needed someone else to talk to other than Him. Jesus surrounded himself with disciples. X-Man when you are looking for a friend, find yourself someone with the characteristics of Nathan or Paul. Find a friend who will love you enough to pray for you and encourage you. Find a friend like Hur, someone who will hold you up when you're tired and weary. Find a friend who loves you enough to stay with you in your time of need, who loves you enough to confront you even when you have done wrong. When you are confronted, ask God for prudence, good judgment, good sense and ability to take correction. Find a friend who will not judge or betray you.

When I practiced Law, everyone in Brookhaven formed an opinion of me and so did I. Obviously, it didn't help that I was arrogant and felt that I was good at what I did. I was an exceptional liar and litigator. There was no case I wouldn't take. There were few lines I would not cross, just because I wanted to win. For my clients, I thought I was a hero, but to God I was just a disobedient kid trying to find his way. I felt like everyone was counting on me and I had to win even if I had to cheat. I wanted to win because I wanted to satisfy the people that hired me. Clients didn't care how far the law got bent they just wanted victory. I learned that finding friends at work was not a good idea and Justice was not blind. All sides were cheating every chance they got. There was no integrity only arrogance and pride. The only person blind was me.

I thought if I won, I would have friends. I thought if I was a success, I would have friends. Everybody judged me by the suits I wore, my office and the car I drove. No one gave two cents about my soul. People were all looking at me from the outside thinking I had it all together, when all the while on the inside, I was struggling. And when my conditions and circumstances began to change, I looked for my friends. Even the people I had helped the most turned against me or were standing afar off watching and waiting to see what my outcome would be. Thank God, Jesus (my friend) never left me alone. In the end, I realized I had very few friends, only acquaintances and co-workers. I realized for the first time, that I had people in my life who meant me no heavenly or earthly good. I had people in my life that hung around me because of my status, but none of them really knew me. Even though I had been a good friend, no one came to me as a friend and said, "Edward, how are you doing? Is there anything you need, can I help in any way? No one reminded me, "Edward you are a child of the King; He is king in every situation. He will stick closer than a brother. He'll be your friend when all others have forsaken you. I had read *Proverbs 18:24* which states; "A man that hath friends must shew himself friendly: and there is a friend that sticketh closer than a brother." I had been a friend, a good friend. I thought God was giving instructions about earthly friendships. I now understand that we must show ourselves friendly to God, through obedience. Thus due to my legal misunderstandings, and in spite of all my past efforts, those alleged friends without ever knowing all the facts of my circumstances, judged and condemned me. But in my secret closet, still a sinner, I prayed to God. I prayed to my friend, but I couldn't give in and surrender all to him. All on the altar, I still would not lay.

X-Man, despite how you may have been treated, be a friend to your brother as Christ has been a friend to you. *Hebrew 3:12-13* states: "take heed, brethren, lest there be in any of you an evil heart of unbelief, in departing from the living God. But exhort one another daily, while it is called Today; lest any of you be hardened through the deceitfulness of sin." We all need encouragement. Unlike in the past, this time God had blessed me and surrounded me with friends. My friend in my greatest time of need was Jesus. God has now given me a new best friend and life companion, my wife Aisha. She knows everything about me and she does not let me slide on anything. We have been able to share our successes and failures. She has been there through some good times and seen me through my roughest hour. She has no problem in confronting me and telling me how she feels. Yet she continues to believe in me as a man of God. She's my cheerleader in every endeavor and when I'm wrong she gets in my face the way Paul did Peter in *Galatians 2:11.*

I've been blessed to have some friends in my life who are never afraid to tell me when I err, and yet encourage me to press forward like Rev. Ronald O. Perry, my present Pastor at Springfield. Good friends will help you confront your mistakes. X-Man a good friends will never leave you or forsake you even when you've done wrong. In my darkest hour when I felt I had no where to turn it was friends like Ren Brown, Natasha Haynes, Charleston Hudson, Luader Smith, J.P. Smith, Glen Brown, Laura Young, Diane Benson, Deborah Benson, Mary Jane Dillon, Larry Gatlin, Raymond Boutwell, Bishop Jerry Durr, Louis Calcolt, Phillip Sterling and Bruce Smith to name a few, who kept me from going into depression; that is what kept me strong and focused on my salvation.

One of the most interesting stories of the bible is the one about David and Batsheba. David had murdered Uriah to cover up his act of adultery with Batsheba. About a year after the murder of Uriah, David was found out. His friend the Prophet Nathan came to confront him about Bathsheba and Uriah. Nathan told David a story about a rich man who had numerous sheep, cattle and lambs and a poor man who had only one ewe lamb. Nathan told David that although the rich man had more than enough, he took the lamb of the poor man to use for his own purpose. At this point the scripture states that David grew angry and stated that the rich man that had done this great injustice should be killed and made to repay fourfold. Nathan told David, "You are the man that has done this deed." When confronted with his sin, David had two choices-the same choices you and I have when we come face to face with our sins. David could confess and repent or become arrogant and self righteous. He could have killed Nathan like Manasseh killed the prophet Isaiah, but he didn't. Instead he heeded the warning and fell on his knees before Nathan and confessed and asked God to have mercy on him and to blot out his transgressions, to wash and cleanse him(see *Ps. 51:1-5).* Thus, even after being found out that he was an adulterous murder, at the end of his life, David was described as a man after God's own heart. X-Man, I hope you're not still wondering if God can use a person like you?

You need some more examples of commitment and friendship, consider other timeless biblical examples such as Jonathan and David or Ruth and Naomi. Both friendships were based on devotion to God and to his principles. The full story of David and Jonathan can be found in the books of *1 and 2 Samuel*. The two men had a great friendship based on mutual commitment sacrifice and mutual humility. Had Jonathan not helped David escape the wrath of Saul, Jonathan would have became King instead of David. If you are wondering how far and to what lengths you should go for a friend, consider David and Jonathan. If you are wondering if your relationship can withstand cultural differences, age and religious differences, consider the story of Ruth and Naomi in the book of Ruth. Naomi had two sons who married two girls from Moad, Orpah and Ruth. And when Naomi's sons died, Orpah went back to Moad, but Ruth remained with Naomi and the two women became friends. Ruth told Naomi "we are family now. Where you go, I go. Your people will be my people! Your God will be my God!" If ever there was an example of love, friendship and commitment it was between these two women. X-Men and women, find yourself a friend.

Whatever you do, do not compromise your salvation—it is not worth it. Remember, God owes you nothing, but an opportunity for salvation. If you have some genuine Christian friends in your life, listen to them because they were sent by God to keep you in check, to keep you strong, to see that you remain an X-Man until the end. If you are searching for friends be sure to size them up. Be sure to get to know their character, find their true personality, motivations and values. Learn if they are cheerful or negative and cynical? Are they unselfish or self-serving? Are they trustworthy or disloyal? Do they gossip about others to you? Do they have a relationship with Jesus Christ? What is the character of the people they currently consider as their friends? Understand that friendship takes work, time, endurance and sacrifice; make sure your efforts are not in vain.

SESSION TWELVE

A Mind Is A Terrible Thing To Waste

X-Man, you have come a long way on your journey. You are no longer afraid, you are an overcoming, qualified X-Man who has accepted his calling and found a friend. The only thing the devil can do to trip up your walk is attack your mind. Being an X-Man does not exempt you from the temptations of this world. Satan shall forever confront you with your unconfessed sin, secret struggles and hidden failures. Even Christ was tempted by Satan, but He never yielded. And now it's your turn. ***A heart committed to Christ and a mind filled with the things of God makes a difficult target for Satan.*** Remember God is faithful and with every temptation he will make a way of escape that you may be able to bear it. ***1 Cor. 10:13.*** Even when Christ was teaching his disciples (X-Men), He encouraged them to pray, "Lead us not into temptation, but deliver us from evil" (*Matt. 6:13*). The key at this point may seem complicated and difficult, but do not quit.

Every person has the challenge of controlling his or her mind. The mind is constantly jumping from one thought to another like a monkey on a tree. The mind is constantly contemplating each various emotions like love, hate, pride, rage, anger, guilt, shame, jealously, envy, doubt and fear. That why God stated to keep our minds stayed on Him. That's why He had ***Matthew*** to write in *6:24*: "No man can serve two masters; for either he will hate the one and love the other; or lese he will hold to one, and despise the other. Ye cannot serve God and mammon." You cannot continue to cling to past hurts or successes or continuously yield to temptation.

Temptation is a mental invitation to do something that is wrong. Thus sin does not take place until we accept the invitation. The old hymn by Horatio R. Palmer says, *"Yield not to temptation, For yielding is sin. Each victory will help you some other to win. Fight manfully onward dark passions subdue, look ever to Jesus he will carry you through. You just ask the savior to help you, comfort, strengthen and keep you. He is willing to aid you. He will carry you through."* Continue your transformation by transforming your mind. "Thus, be ye transformed by the renewing of your mind. Let this mind be in you which was also in Christ Jesus" (*Philippians 2:5*). In order to make a complete transformation from who you were to who God is calling you to be you need to renew your mind. Do you remember watching the superhero cartoons when you were a kid? Whenever the world was in trouble, ordinary citizens would say some special words, run into an alley or a telephone booth and come out as the Super Hero. People they worked with and lived with daily did not know that the super hero and their friend were one and the same person. I could never believe that Lois Lane did not know that Clark Kent was Super Man and that Mary Jane never figured out that Peter Parker was Spiderman. I tell you when God gets through dealing with you, everyone will notice a difference and will no longer see the old you. They will see an X-Man a New Creature, who by the grace and power of Christ comes to recruit and draw other sinners to him who can save their souls. They will see the newly transformed and evolved you.

It is ironic that we call a person who has spent time in jail an ex-convict? As I stated earlier, Peter, Paul, Silas and Daniel to name a few were x-cons and Moses was a fleeing felon. Our saints and prophets who were imprisoned never allowed their minds to be a holding cell for sin. They did not wallow in self-pity. Just like these guys, as an X-Man you are a prisoner of Christ, willingly held captive by God's loving spirit, and confined to His word and his way. *Ephesians 4:1* Paul states: "I therefore, the prisoner of the Lord, beseech you that ye walk worthy of the vocation wherewith ye are called." X-Man to be a prisoner for Christ is a privilege that accentuates your love for and commitment to Christ as a willing servant.

Don't think your calling into ministry means prosperity and the absence of trial, testing and suffering. As X-Men we engage in a constant mental wrestling match between who we were and who we are in Christ. Apostle Paul wrote, "When I want to do good, evil is right there with me" *(Romans 7:21).* Do whatever you have to do, but do not give up the fight. Be like Jacob and wrestle God for your blessing if you have to. Wrestle until you get a break through. Do not become unstable or make excuses. Be steadfast and unmovable. Persevere through your trials for there is a blessing coming at the break of day. "And Jacob was left alone; and there wrestled a man with him until the breaking of the day" *(Genesis 32:24).* "And he said, thy name shall be called no more Jacob, but Israel: for you have struggled with God and with men, and prevailed." **Genesis 32:28**. Wrestle until your name is changed to X-Man. X-Man do not let God go until He blesses you.

> *You cannot persevere unless there is a trial in your life. There can be no victories without battles; there can be no peaks without valleys. If you want the blessings you must be prepared to carry the burden and fight the battle. God has to balance privileges with responsibilities, blessings with burdens, or else you and I become spoiled pampered children.*
>
> *Warren Wiersbe.*

Remember how Jacob grew up spoiled and deceitful. God does not need pampered children—He needs men. Jacob was worried about his impending meeting with his brother Esau. He did not know if Esau was coming as a friend or as an enemy. All he knew, all he could think about, was that his brother was coming and he was bringing 400 men with him. Jacob knew after all he had done to his brother, that he couldn't face him without a blessing from God—so he wrestled.

In case you still haven't figured it out, being an X-Man is hard work. It requires endurance, patience and commitment. It requires you to get back up each time you fall. So what if you are struggling with discouragement? Become your own cheerleader! Don't let the devil control your thoughts, for he will also control your peace and your joy. Be like David when he came to Ziglag and saw that the city had been burned and the people had been taken away captive. All of the soldiers' spirits were trampled with grief with only David to blame. After falling to his knees crying about what he had lost, David remembered who his God was and is. *I tell you a mind is a terrible thing to waste, for redemption lies in remembrance.* David remembered he was a man after God's own heart. He remembered God told him that although he may walk in the valley and shadow of death, he was to fear no evil, for God would be with him. As a result, David stood up, dust himself off and encouraged himself to pursue and recover what had been taken from him.

In *Samuel 30:6 and 8* it states: "and David was greatly distressed; for the people spake of stoning him, because the soul of all the people was grieved, every man for his sons and for his daughters: but David encouraged himself in the Lord his God [. . .] And David inquired of the Lord saying, shall I pursue after this troop? Shall I overtake them? And He answered him, Pursue: for thou shalt surely overtake them, and without fail recover all." X-Man maybe you've lost your family and you want it back; I encourage you to pursue, overtake and recover all. Maybe your life is on the verge of destruction, I challenge you to overtake and recover all. Maybe you've been divorced, (there is a reason the person you divorced is called your x-wife or x-husband) get up, get over it and get on with your life. Maybe your career has been taken from you. If you still desire it—pursue it and recover all. Maybe you have lost your manhood—given way to alternative life styles—it is not too late to pursue, overtake and recover all. Maybe you've been a dead beat dad; it is not too late to pursue and recover all. Maybe you have a criminal background, committed adultery, have bad credit, have been dishonest, are an alcoholic, drug addict, sex addict, or a gambler, just remember whose son you are: encourage yourself, pursue, overtake and recover all.

Get mentally focused and transform your mind. Before you can conquer you have to believe that you can. Victory starts in your mind. When the devil wants to get to you, he attacks your mind. Victory as an X-Man requires persistence in your walk with the Lord.

> "*Nothing in the world can take the place of persistence. Talent will not; nothing in the world is more common than unsuccessful men with talent. Genius will not; unrewarded genius is a proverb. Education will not; the world is full of educated derelicts. Persistence and determination alone are omnipotent . . .*"

Calvin Coolidge, thirtieth President of the United States

X-Men are persistent men. X-Men are persistent in their prayer life. X-Men are persistent and their destinations certain. Giving up and quitting are words not found in the vocabulary of X-Men. X-Men are faithful and determined. Despite the obstacles ahead, X-Men will not stop until they reach their ultimate goal of seeing Jesus face to face. X-Men endure the trials of life as Jesus endured the cross. *2 Timothy 2:3-4* declares "thou therefore endure hardness, as a good soldier of Jesus Christ. No man that warreth, entangleth himself with the affairs of this life, that he may please Him who chose him to be a soldier. X-Man whatever you do, don't quit. Your transformation is not over until God calls you home to be with Him. In the interim, X-Men will have to endure.

Life is a gift, so live it as such. You will have an eternity to figure out what you did with it your life. We are all transiting through this earth for a brief while, but God has offered us the priceless gift of eternal life through His son Jesus Christ. I beseech you to run this race to the end, run with the intent to win, mentally visualize the finish line and get back up each time you fall. Become a construction contractor on your own life. If something breaks, fix it. If you see a crack in the foundation of your relationship, fix it. Drill out the decay and pour in some fresh cement. If you are not all you should be, remodel and add onto your life. If you are not filled with the living water, work on your plumbing or dig a new Well. If you are still weighed down from old mess, fix your sewage and flush it out of your life. Study the word and strengthen your foundation. Get up renewed and refreshed, because you are an X-Man-and your mind is a terrible thing to waste.

This is your life you are dealing with. Do not let the devil attack your mind. Present yourself to Christ as a living sacrifice unto God, which is your reasonable service. For yourself, your creator and for everyone you encounter in this life, be an X-Man. If you know someone living in sin, remember they are still loved by God, as you yourself were once a sinner, now saved by grace. In this highly competitive world with constant demands and expectations, I know you may have been discouraged, misunderstood and slandered, but know that you have been called according to God's purpose. When faced with the trials of life and you have hope mingled with pain, you cannot give up. When the world has thrown you in the Lion's Den, you cannot quit. When confronted with a fiery furnace experience, know that God is well able to deliver you. When Goliath is staring you down in the valley, put on the whole Armor of God run toward your enemy and fight with all your might.

If you have found yourself and you realize you are not the man God wants you to be, you can change right now. If you are striving daily to be the best man you can be, I implore you to stop, surrender, face your sins, confess and correct them. I heard a joke once: How many psychologists does it takes to change a light bulb? Answer, just one. But the light bulb has to want to be changed. I know that each person reading this book has the ability to make some changes in his or her life. How many saviors does it take to change and transform you? Just one, but you have to want to change. As Vance Havner is quoted as saying, "Life is a series of choices between the bad, the good, and best. Everything depends on how we choose." In light of the above, you, and only you, must, "Choose for yourself this day whom you will serve. As for me and my household, we will serve the Lord" (*Joshua 24:15*). When you are losing hope in the midst of adversity, surrounded by temptation, weary, worn and torn, heartbroken, frustrated, or on the verge of giving up, look to God and He will lift you up. God and only God is the author and finisher of your faith. So have some faith in Him and make a change.

The difference between your success and failure as an X-Man is in your mind. The bible says: "so as a man thinketh so is he." If you are stuck in a rut, and feel unfulfilled change your thinking. If you are looking to find new friends, develop relationships, walk in your calling, find a better job, become financially secure and have the life that God wants you to have, then change your thinking. As long as you pray and keep control of your mind you can face any obstacle, have inner peace and climb the tallest mountain. When you have peace of mind, you can eliminate stress from your life, increase your self-confidence, program yourself for success and boost your self-esteem. When your mind is free and your thinking is steadfast on Christ, your entire life is brand new, you are a new creature. When you have your mind on Jesus, you can stop being ruled by your past. When you have your mind on Jesus, you can set a path for victory and eliminate your fears. When your mind is on Jesus, regardless of your situation, He will come and show you the way out.

A man walking down the street on a sidewalk fell into an uncovered man hole. The man was stuck, bruised and couldn't get out. He began to scream and cry out for help as people walked by. Finally, a preacher walked by and after hearing the man's cry, the preacher wrote out a scripture and dropped it down to the man for encouragement. A few hours later a doctor heard the man cry out and as he walked by, he wrote out a prescription for pain and dropped it down to the man. The man continued to cry out for help and finally another man heard his cry looked down in the man hole and jumped down into the hole with him. The man who had fallen asked "why did you jump down here with me, for now we are both stuck?" The other man replied, *"don't worry, I've been down here before and I know the way out."* Maybe you know of a man or woman who is not the best they can be. Maybe you can identify with their pain, praise, struggle and even their triumphs. Be a beacon light that shows them the way out of their situation. Give them a copy of this book as they examine themselves and remind them that their outlook is not hopeless. "Without God, we cannot. Without us, God will not" (*St. Augustine*). In the end, when I did not believe He would, God used me. I believe God can and will use you and no devil in hell or on earth is going to take that blessing away: it is your birthright.

For I am persuaded, that neither death, nor life, nor angels, nor principalities, nor powers, nor things present, nor things to come, Nor height, nor depth, nor any other creature, shall be able to separate us from the love of God, which is in Christ Jesus our Lord (*Romans 8:38-39*). X-Men until the end. Amen.

CONCLUSION

X-Man I pray that you now understand who and whose you are. You cried, you died, you fell in love. Despite your fear, you've been qualified and justified and found fit for service. You have overcome the struggles of life and accepted your calling. You have found a friend and transformed your mind. So now, here we are—the conclusion of the matter. God said, "No one, having put his hand to the plow and looking back is fit for the Kingdom of God" (*Luke 9:62*). You cannot go AWL (Absent Without Leave) and expect to get into the Kingdom. So what are God's final words for X-Men as we embark on each day equipped to challenge the unknown? "Finally, brethren, whatsoever things are true, whatsoever things are honest, whatsoever things are pure, whatsoever things are lovely, whatsoever things are of good report; if there be any virtue, and if there be any praise, think on these things. Those things, which ye have both learned, and received, and heard, and seen in me, do: and the God of peace shall be with you. But rejoice in the Lord greatly, that now at the last your care of me hath flourished again; wherein ye were also careful, but lacked opportunity. Not that I speak in respect of want: for I have learned, in whatsoever state I am, therewith to be content" (*Philippians 4:8-11*). I can finally be content in knowing that I am an X-Man. I pray that you can to. After all of God's profound spiritual lessons, I now know whom my soul loves. I believe we all know to some degree how to be abased and abound, to be full and to be hungry and to suffer need. But, nevertheless, whatever your calling, know that you can do all things through Christ which strengthens you. Hang in there, be of good courage for God has not forgotten you. X-Man, the Christ-Man. Now you know the answer to your life's equation, come join the evolution of man.

Now that you have re-evaluated your goals, adjusted your career and put God in the equation; now that you can see the big picture and plan for contingencies; now that you can see life through eyes of hope, love and forgiveness. Now that you understand that both men and women needs to receive caring, respect, devotion, validation and reassurance. Now that you have a new level of awareness and are evolving into an X-Man, don't fall into the devil's trap and get full of pride again. *Proverbs 16:18* says, "pride goeth before destruction." Do not get sucked in, blinded and fooled by pride; avoid it daily by prayer. Do not get so comfortable with your walk with Christ that you begin to feel you can do your own thing. Stay focused on God and your walk until you take your last breath. Do not flinch, wink or even blink away from Him. Do not join the ranks of Uzziah and Judas Iscariot. Do not miss your final transformation to heaven.

> *"Many of life's failures are people who did not realize how close they were to success when they gave up."*

> *Thomas A. Edison.*

In *2 Chronicles 26*, we learn the story of King Uzziah who was sixteen years old when he became King of Judah and he reigned for fifty-two years in Jerusalem. For almost fifty-two years, Uzziah was an excellent X-Man. He loved and followed God and he was blessed by God until he became strong and full of pride. After fifty-two years, he became blinded by pride and died in his sins as an outcast leper. After fifty-two years, he became comfortable and thought he could do his own thing. Do not follow Uzziah's path, spending 52 years as an X-Man and then giving up. Don't join God's army only to receive a Dishonorable Discharge after all your years of service. Judas started out as an X-Man (disciple) of Jesus Christ, but he betrayed Jesus for thirty 30 pieces of silver and a kiss. He later hanged himself. You have come too far to throw in the towel. What a terrible way to go out, to have walked with Christ only to get so caught up that it costs you your very soul.

Unlike the reality show Survivor and the Amazing Race, where you win the challenge of holding out and finishing the race of life as an X-Man or X-Woman, the prize is much greater than winning One Million Dollars and a new car. The grand prize for each winner in Christ is eternal life. Yes, everyone can be a winner. The down side to not taking advantage of God's amazing grace and surviving this amazing transformation race in Christ is that the losers do not get the luxury of enjoying temporary notoriety for having participated in the game. The penalty for losing is the wages of sin—Death. Do not continue a life sentence on Death Row. Change your circle of death to a circle of life, because losers get no consolation prize of eternity in Heaven, for their destination is hell. Surely, you don't want to be the "Big Fat Loser"!

Remember in your pursuit for a complete transformation, X-Man, you do not go alone. You are apart of the winning team. You are a member of the Fantastic Four. You ought to know by now that I don't mean Mr. Fantastic, the Thing, the Human Torch or Invisible Girl. You are a member of the original superhero team, the one assembled at creation, the Father, the Son, the Holy Ghost and the man created in their image and likeness, X-Man. Whatever you do, do not forget your calling into ministry. Make sure that you are living the example of the hero that lives inside of you. "Let no corrupt communication proceed out of your mouth, but that which is good to the use of edifying that it may minister grace unto the heavens. And grieve not the Holy Spirit of God, whereby ye are sealed unto the day of redemption. Let all bitterness, and wrath, and anger, and clamour, and evil speaking, be put away from you, with all malice: And be ye kind one to another, tenderhearted, forgiving one another, even as God for Christ's sake hath forgiven you" (*Ephesians 4:29-32*). As an X-Man, you need to be steadfast and unmovable and always abounding in the word of God.

No matter the obstacle, regardless of the hardship, don't digress from your new path—keep your eyes on the finish line. I remember an incident that occurred while I was attending Copiah-Lincoln Community College and running track. I was running the second leg on the mile relay team which is usually the last event of most track meets in Mississippi and often the deciding event between teams that are close in points for overall first place. As I was turning the curve coming into the home stretch, the runner in the next lane tripped me: I fell down and rolled over as I got trampled. I got up despite my bruises and continued to run the race. My team still won the race and set the track meet record that day. Our coach told me that initially he was ready to run out onto the field as he believed the race was over and that I had quit. He said it was the first time he ever saw a runner trip, fall, rollover, get up, finish the race with no break in stride. As I look back, I could have quit, I could have stayed down, but I was determined not to let my teammates down. I was determined to finish what I had started. X-Man, there will be times in your life, maybe even now, when the devil will try to trip you. I encourage you, despite your bruises, to never break your stride, but to roll over, get up, and finish the race: victory is within your sights. As the songwriter wrote: [X-Men]*"You have come this far by faith. Leaning on the Lord. Your have been trusting in His holy word; (and) He never failed you yet. Can't turn around, you've come too far by faith."*. . . *Well (as an X-Man) I can truly say; the Lord will make away, because He never failed me yet. That's why I'm (still singing); I can't turn around, we've come this far by faith."*

The greatest words of triumph ever sounded in the ears of man were those spoken by Christ on the Cross: "It is finished!" (*John 19:30*). Those were the final words spoken in the redemption of mankind. God has left you His spirit because of your obedience toward Him (*Acts 5:32*). Do not quench the Spirit or throw away your special friendship (*1 Thes 5:19*). Quench means to put out, to stop. Do not quench God's spirit in you by falling back into sin. Your conversion is not your salvation, it is just the beginning of your new walk as an X-Man. A walk that requires continued obedience to God. "Behold I shew you a mystery; We shall not all sleep, but we shall all be changed, in a moment, in the twinkling of an eye, at the last trumpet: for the trumpet shall sound, and the dead shall be raised incorruptible, and we shall be changed. For this corruptible must put on incorruption, and this mortal must put on immortality" (*1 Corinthians 15:51-53*). At the last trumpet sound announcing the return of Christ, we who died in Christ shall undergo our final transformation. On the last trumpet sound your evolution shall be complete. "Therefore, my beloved brethren, be ye steadfast, unmovable, always abounding in the work of the Lord, forasmuch as ye know that your labour is not in vain in the Lord" (*1 Corinthians 15:58*). X-Man, do not go fifty-two years only for your labour to be in vain. Upon the final review of your life I pray you are able to say, without reservation or regret, "I have fought a good fight." You need to make it in on the final transformation, because I have read that eyes have not seen nor ears heard what the Lord has in store for the X-Men who love Him. One of these days, "God will wipe away every tear from your eyes; there shall be no more death, nor sorrow, nor crying" (*Revelations 21:4*). X-Man, hang in there, for His glory. Finish your calling as an X-Man, be like Apostle Paul, fight a good fight and finish your course—for you are the evolution of man, **A NEW ANOINTED CREATURE OF CHRIST**.

X-MAN: GOD'S NEW CREATURE

BY: EDWARD O. BENSON

**"If any man be in Christ, he is a new creature [X-Man]; old things
are passed away; behold, all things have become new"
(2 Corinthians 5:17)**

X-MAN STUDY GUIDE

*Study to show thy self approved to be an "X-Man"
rightly dividing the word of truth.*

X-MAN DEFINED

X-Man: A Christ-Man. A Man of God; A New Creature in Christ; A Man who
had put aside his sins to follow Christ; Men who are evolving themselves daily to
becoming a new man in Christ; Men who have transformed their character and
behavior and accepted their calling to work and recruit for Christ. An anointed
Man of God.

PURPOSE OF STUDY GUIDE

Start an X-Man study group at your church and create a since of brotherhood
with your fellow believers where each of you can endure, sweat, bleed, cry, pray and
praise together. Each session of questions are relevant to the sessions of the text of
the book. For those questions that do not have a biblical reference, you can get that
information from the session of the text. Other questions are for discussion and to
get you thinking about your own conversion and transformation.

SESSION ONE

The Transformation Begins
A New Creature In Christ

1.   What do you think about when you see the letter X?
2.   What is the X in your life?
3.   At this point what do you think it means to be an X (Christ)-Man?
4.   If you were to define your present walk with Jesus, how would you describe yourself?
5.   What do you think about when you read 1 Corinthians 9:27?
6.   Who was your favorite hero, and why?
7.   Where do you see yourself in Ministry?
8.   What does it mean to be transformed in Christ?
9.   How long does the transformation take?
10. What is your mission statement for living? Write out your mission statement and explain why you chose the words you used.
11. What does it mean to be a new creature? 2 Cor. 5:17.
12. What does it mean to be born again and given a new heart? John 3:3-8; 1 Peter 1:3, 23; Ezek.11:19; also Deut.30:5, 6.
13. What does Proverbs 27:19 mean to you?
14. What do I have to do to be saved? John 3:3.
15. Who is God? Acts 17:23
16. Is everyone convicted by the truth?

SESSION TWO

Is It Alright To Cry?
Big Boys Don't Cry!

1.   What motivates you to live the life you live?
2.   Do you have anxiety about changing your life?
3.   When was the last time you cried?
4.   What do you tell your children when they cry?
5.   What happened in your life that was too humiliating to forget?
6.   How have you been taught to deal with your emotions?
7.   When was the last time you got angry?
8.   What is the difference between a man growing up in Christ and growing old in Christ?

9. What happened in your life that was so emasculating that it took you away from God?
10. How would you describe your personality?
11. What is the biggest difference between you and your spouse regarding the expression of emotions?
12. Does the Holy Spirit demonstrate emotion and exercise will? See Romans15:30; 1 Corinthians 12:11 and 1 Thess. 5:19
13. Give some specific instances in the bible where Jesus expressed emotion?
14. What does God say about our tears? Revelations 7:17; also see Revelations 21:4
15. When it comes to showing emotions, what is a man supposed to do?
16. Do women feel that men don't listen and are emotionally unavailable?
17. Do men feel that women are always trying to change them?
18. Who is the only person capable a making a lasting change in the life of Men?

SESSION THREE

A Time To Die.
"If you haven't found something to die for, you are not fit to live."

1. Is there someone in your family that you need to call and tell them you love them?
2. When you die, what will be your epitaph?
3. What will be the verdict on your life on Judgment day?
4. Doing eternity what will you be able to say you did with your life that truly had lasting value?
5. For the living know that they shall die, so what are you going to do? (Ecclesiastics: 9:5)
6. If you could write your own obituary, what would it say?
7. In Luke 9:23 what do you think God meant when He said deny yourself?
8. What does it mean to take up your cross?
9. Are you ready for the suffering, trials and pain of ministry? Why or why not?
10. Why is it important to seek God while He may be found?
11. How many times like Peter have you denied Christ?
12. What are you seeking God for?
13. What does John 12:24-25 teach us about the benefits of dying in Christ?
14. What are some of the things you feel you need to die to?
15. How many times will you suffer a physical death? See Hebrew 9:27
16. What did Jesus Die for?
17. Does the church need healing?
18. Does the Church need to die before it Dies?

SESSION FOUR

Master Can You Use Me?
"So what if you've broken all Ten Commandments?"

1.   What in the world would you want more than a relationship with God?
2.   What is your god?
3.   Do you believe God can use you?
4.   What do you feel that has happened in your life that makes you wonder if God can use you?
5.   What is your favorite commandment?
6.   In reference to your answer above, why did you pick this particular commandment?
7.   In Isaiah 43:19, What do you think God meant when he said he was going to do a New thing?
8.   How old was Moses when he fled Egypt?
9.   How old was Moses when left Midian to return to Egypt?
10. How long did Moses' Ministry last?
11. What was the significance of Moses' Death?
12. When was the last time you invited someone to church?
13. Can I live a Christian life? Matt.5:8
14. What is the trinity? 2 Cor. 13:14
15. If I sin, will I lose my salvation? See Hebrew 6:4-6
16. What is the present day application of the Ten commandments?
17. How does your answer take into account the application of Romans 6:14 which states Christians are not under law, but under grace? (See also Deut.4:13; Deut 9:9-11; Ex. 34:27-28)
18. Will a nation of God-fearing people be better off than a nation without God? (See Proverbs 29:2)

SESSION FIVE

Who Are You Trying To Impress?
"Dress to Impress"

1.   What do you have or possess that's worth going to Hell for?
2.   How did you grow from your failures?
3.   Who are you still trying to impress?
4.   When you went on your last job interview, what were some of the questions the interviewer asked?

5.   What are you reaching for in God?
6.   What kind of impression will your lifestyle leave on your family and future generations?
7.   What kind of impression has God made on you?
8.   Why should you not worry about impressing man?
9.   What is your opinion of the prodigal son story?
10.   What about his life would make someone want to nickname him prodigal?
11.   Why was his brother not as happy for him as his father was when he came home?
12.   Have you made your decision to come home?
13.   Who have you lived for to get their approval, appreciation and affection?
14.   When Adam messed up who was and is ruler over the earth? See Genesis 1:26; See also Luke 4:5-7
15.   Did God know Adam would sin before He created him?
16.   When did God know he would have to send Jesus to die for our Sins?
17.   Can we earn favor of God, by our good works?
18.   It is said that we learn by example. If this is true, then what do you think the boys in your church or your son will learn from watching your life?
19.   Consider the ideas of hypocrisy and judgment discussed in Matthew 7:1-5.
20.   Why do you feel men are described as aggressive, combative and territorial? Is this description a good thing?

SESSION SIX

When An X-man Falls In Love
"Love covers a multitude of Faults"

1.   Is Christ worthy of your love?
2.   Are you worthy of His?
3.   How would you define love?
4.   How would you define commitment?
5.   What does it mean to Love God with all your heart, soul and mind? See Matthew 22:37-40.
6.   We all would like for Jesus to crash through the sky and say: "This is my beloved son with whom I am well pleased." If God crashed through the sky right now, what do you think He would say about you?
7.   If you had to describe your Christian experience in twelve words or less what would you say or write?
8.   Where were you when you finally let God in?
9.   How did you first come to know the Savior?
10.   How far away from God has your sin taken you?

11. How long have you stayed in a sinful situation before letting it go?
12. What did the situation or sin represented above cost you?
13. What does 1 Corinthians 14:1 teach us regarding pursuing love?
14. How does the lack of love relate to your spiritual death? 1 John 3:14
15. What does it mean to be counted worthy of the Kingdom? 2 Thes 1:3
16. Is it possible to be saved and yet be considered unworthy of the Kingdom? 2 Thes. 5, 11
17. How does the world define love?
18. How is love shown or expressed?
19. How did God show His love for us? (See 1 Cor. 13; Romans 5:6; 8:34; 1 Peter 3:18.)
20. If God loves you so much why does He allow you to suffer?
21. What has God's love done for you?
22. Read Jonah 4:11 what does it say about God's love?
23. What promise is given in Psalm 91:14?
24. Can you do anything to cause God to stop loving you?
25. What are the effects of love? Proverbs 3:3; 21:21.

SESSION SEVEN

Be Afraid-Be Very Afraid!
"If you're scared, just say you're scared."

1. What do you need from God?
2. Do you feel God will give you what you ask, Why or Why not?
3. How do you define fear?
4. Have you ever been afraid of something or someone?
5. Why should you not worry?
6. What have you done that God does not know about? Proverbs 15:3
7. What kind of spirit has God placed in you?
8. What is human nature?
9. What type of men will God give His Spirit to?
10. What did Jesus mean when He said it is finished? See John 19:30 and Hebrews 10:10-18
11. What does it mean to not be afraid to fail?
12. How can your failures help advance the gospel of Christ?
13. What failures did Paul mention in Philippians 3:13-14 and how do they apply to you?

SESSION EIGHT

Qualified And Justified?
Who's In Control: Pride, Repentance, And Humility?

1. What kind man do you want to be?
2. Pick a man in the bible and discuss why you think he is an X-Man?
3. Discuss whether or not he went to heaven when he died, why or why not?
4. Describe his character before he encountered God and compare it to his character after he encountered God?
5. Describe things about the man you chose that are most similar to your character?
6. What qualifies you for service in God's army?
7. What are God's promises to the humble? Ps. 138:6, Isa 66:2, Luke 9:48, 14:11, James 4:6 and 1 Peter 5:5.
8. How would you describe Christ's humility? Mt. 11:29, Zech. 9:9, John 13:5, 2 Cor.8: 9, Php. 2:8, Mt. 20:28, Mt. 13:55, John 9:29, Isa. 50:6, 53:7, Acts 8:32, Mt. 26:37-39, John 10:15, 17, 18; and Heb.12: 2
9. What do you think about the life of Manasseh? See 2 King 21:1-17 and 2 Chronicles 33?
10. Why do you think God restored Manasseh back to his Kingdom?
11. Like Bartimaeus what are you screaming out to God for?
12. Has God answered your scream for help?
13. How can we overcome Satan? See Revelations 12:11
14. Why did Jonah say out of the belly of hell, cried I? See Jonah 2:1
15. Was Jonah ever cast out of God's sight?
16. Describe what Jonah 2:5 means to you?
17. What is the greatest virtue? Matt. 18:1-4
18. What is the meaning of the phrase, "Justified God," in Luke 7:29? How is it different from our justification?
19. How does one become qualified to receive the blessing, which God has promised to give those who are Abraham's children? Romans 1:18-4:25
20. What does it mean to be qualified for baptism and in whose name shall a person be baptized? Contrast Matt. 28:18-20 with Acts 2:38 and Col. 2:9 and Luke 24:47.
20. What does it mean to be morally justified to do something?
21. How shall the just in Christ live?
22. Discuss Proverbs 29:23; Micah 6:8; Matthew 18:4; James 4:6; 1 Peter 5:6 and Proverbs 6:16-17.

INTERLUDE

"The Power of Twelve—A Prophetic Number"

1. What is the significance of the numbers in your life?
2. Have you surrendered to the word of God?
3. Maybe it has taken you only one or two years to accept your calling, research the numbers one and two.
4. Pick one of the numbers and research it: 3, 6, 7, 10, and 40?
5. How do you feel about the number twelve as a prophetic number?
6. Why do you think God allowed the author run for twelve years?
7. What do you feel was the significance of Jesus speaking in the temple at age twelve?
8. Why did Jesus have only twelve Apostles?
9. Why did the woman have an issue of blood for twelve years?
10. Why was the damsel he raised from the dead twelve years old?
12. Why does the number twelve represent the congregation of the church?

SESSION NINE

Overcoming The Struggles Of Life
"Life is easy, living is Hard"

1. How have you presented yourself to God? Romans 12:1-3
2. Has God ever not been with you-even in the fire? Daniel 3:24-25
3. What have you done to show God's power to someone this week?
4. Have you ever let fleshly opinions and earthly circumstances hinder your pursuit of God?
5. According to Proverbs 3:5-6 what should a doer of the word be doing?
6. In order to be an effective doer what should X-Men do? See Luke 18:1 also Hosea 4:16
7. List five of your failures and discuss why you think you failed?
8. List five of your successes and discuss why you think you were successful?
9. Do you have great self-esteem and self-confidence?
10. Do you believe in yourself?
11. What were the greatest accomplishments of Mary Magdalene in your opinion?
12. Why does God say you are an overcomer?
13. How would you spend the rest of your life if you knew it was only to last another week? What if you had five years? What if you had another twenty years?
14. How did Joseph deal with the struggles of life after being sold by his brothers?

15. As an X-Man what does it mean to be an overcoming Christian?
16. What characteristics have you recognized that someone you know has been growing in that you have come to appreciate?
17. What is detrimental about experiencing few difficulties in life?
18. What kind of church would my church be if every member were just like me?

SESSION TEN

Do You Believe In Superman?
A Man With A Calling?

1. Do you know what God has called you to do?
2. Are you a man without a calling?
3. How often should an X-Man pray?
4. Will your life have an eternal meaning?
5. Why is it important for you to bear your cross?
6. Why did Jesus pray in the garden to let the cup pass?
7. What does your tomorrow hold?
8. How does your tomorrow affect how you live today?
9. Why do you think Jesse forgot to invite David to eat dinner with Samuel?
10. What do you feel will be the greatest obstacle for you as you walk in your calling?
11. A Calling calls one into leadership. What does 1 Timothy 3:4-5; 5:8 say about leaders?
12. What do you feel is required for Christian leadership?
13. What is one thing a leader cannot delegate?
14. What is the primary obligation of a leader?
15. If you were to rate your self on walking fully in your calling from a scale of 1 (poor) to 10 (excellent), what would you rate yourself?
16. Why didn't Samuel know that David was the one that God wanted and thus ask for him as soon as he got to Jesse's house?
17. What does 1 Peter 5:1-4 tells us about how an X-man should lead?
18. How do you compare to the description of leadership?
19. What can we learn about leadership from reading Mark 9:35; Matthew 20:26-28?
20. How does your career allow room for your calling?
21. What was the first thing Jesus taught his Disciples regarding leadership? See Mark 1:17-18. Why is this important to X-Men?
22. What must an X-Man do once he has been called? See 1 Cor. 7:24
23. Why do you belong to God? 1 Cor.6:20 and 1 Cor.7:23
24. What does Esther 4:14 mean about being called "for such a time as this?"
25. How can I know God's Will? Romans 12:2

SESSION ELEVEN

A Friend Like No Other
"A friend in need is a friend in deed"

1. What are people's perception of you?
2. How many people are in your life that have no genuine interest in your soul?
3. What are you doing regarding the people you just mentioned?
4. Name three people you consider to be a friend?
5. Why do you call them friend?
6. Have you ever been betrayed by someone you consider a friend?
7. Have you ever gotten mad with a friend because the friend confronted you about your sin?
8. Are there people in your life that you have hurt and not asked for forgiveness?
9. Have you asked God who belongs in your life?
10. Who is guarding your heart?
11. Does someone you know need encouragement? Do you need to show yourself friendly?
12. When was the last time you repented and asked God for forgiveness?
13. Do you want unhindered communication with Christ?
14. Do you want unhindered worship with Christ?
15. What else is there in your life you need to separate from?
16. How do you think Nathan felt about going to talk to David?
17. What does Hebrews 3:12-13 say about friendship?
18. What were some of the consequences of David's sin that Nathan confronted him about?
19. Why do you think God waited twelve months before exposing David's sin?
20. Why did Paul confront Peter in Galatians 2:11?
21. How do I forgive my enemies? Matt. 5:43-44
22. How can you tell if you are a part of a true friendship? Consider the following: 1 Samuels 18:3; Romans 12:10; Proverbs 17:17; John 15:13; Psalm 41:9; Hebrew 13:5 and Ephesians 4:32.

SESSION TWELVE

"A mind is a terrible thing to waste"

1. When was the last time you had some serious alone time with God?
2. When was your last break through?
3. What does your name mean?
4. Are you living up to its meaning?

5. Why was changing Jacob's name so important?
6. Could Jacob have walked in his calling without a name change?
7. What does it mean to be sealed until the day of redemption?
8. What does it mean to not grieve the Holy Spirit?
9. When was the last time you encouraged yourself?
10. What does it mean to endure hardness as a soldier for Christ?
11. Is there anything separating you from the love of God?
12. Are you content with you life? Why or why not?
13. What does it means to abide and remain in Jesus? See John 15:1-8
14. How would you classify yourself as an Agent of transformation?
15. How would you define yourself as an X-Man?
16. How do I handle recurring Temptations?
17. How does Hebrews 10:24-25 help us in dealing with Temptation?
18. Why is it important to hide God's word in your heart? Psalm 199:9 & 11.
19. What does James 1:13-18 teach us about temptation and God's plan?
20. What does Romans 3:23 teach us about our battle with Temptation?

CONCLUSION

1. If you died today and were standing before God and He asked, "Why should I let you into My heaven?" What would you say?
2. Now having read this book are you going to continue to live as you have?
3. Are you ready and willing to accept His Gift of eternal life?
4. What specific thing or passage in this book do you feel was the most helpful in your walk with Christ?
5. What things do we contribute to Uzziah's success as a King?
6. Is there any way that Uzziah could have gotten back into God's good grace after the incident with the priest?
7. Is fear a factor for you?
8. Are you a survivor for Christ?
9. Has reading this book helped you in any way?
10. What is salvation?
11. What is real faith?
12. What is the difference between conversion and transformation?
13. What will Satan work in the last days, and who will he deceive? See 2 Thessalonians 2:8-10
14. What can we expect from God upon our final transformation?
15. What can we learn from Isaiah 40:31 that teaches us not to give up as X-Men?
16. When will there come a time when screaming out to the Lord won't matter? See Matt. 7:21
17. What is the unpardonable sin? Matt.12:31
18. When is Jesus coming again? Matt. 24:42
19. What is the greatest sin? Matt. 23:2-12

REFERENCES

All Bible references are taken from The New Scofield Study Bible Authorized King James Version.

Teardrops by Hope Smith
True Transformation by Sr. Kathleen Nealon, CSR.
Love By Grace by Jan McIntosh
Quote from Laura Young
God Give Us Men by Josiah Gilbert Holland
Life's Struggles by Heart Soul Group
Don't Be Afraid To Fail by Author Unknown
Friends by Brittani Kokko
Quote from Warren Wiersbe
Quote from Calvin Coolidge
Quote from Thomas A. Edison
Quote from St. Augustine
Quote Vance Hanner
Quote from Speech of President Bill Clinton on September 11, 1998

ABOUT THE AUTHOR

Edward O'Neal Benson is the youngest of twelve children born in Wesson, Mississippi, raised in Brookhaven, and now resides in Beacon, New York. He is a man born into sin and shaped in iniquity who has struggled with self-examination, self-fulfillment and self-expression in his walk with Christ. He is like so many others born into sin whose coming to Christ was the result of a lot of running, kicking and screaming. He is a simple man who was forced to look into his heart and face God with genuine repentance of his sins and now accepts and walks in his calling.

Edward O'Neal Benson is a man whose soul has been touched by God and molded into a new person, stronger and bolder through the redeeming blood of Jesus Christ. He is the X-Man who has been called of God to recruit you to join the evolution. Edward's mission statement is: because my entire existence is based on charity (God's unconditional love), "May my return gift to God, be my walking in my calling, for submitting my life to Christ is my reasonable service."

If this book has been a blessing to you, share a copy with someone else. Finally, if you have not yet done so, run to the altar; fall on your knees and scream, "Master can you use me?"

If you have an X-Man or X-Woman transformation story that you would like to share, or if you would like to schedule Minister Edward Benson as a speaker: write X-Man Ministries, Inc. Post Office Box 723; Beacon, New York, 12508. We would love to hear from you. Also, you can email us at *Edward@x-menministries.com*